The True Spirit
of the Perpetual Adorers

Catherine-Mectilde de Bar
(1614–1698)

The True Spirit
of the Perpetual Adorers
of the Most Holy Sacrament
of the Altar

✝

Mother Mectilde
of the Blessed Sacrament

Translated by
a Benedictine Oblate

Foreword by
Msgr. Arthur Burton Calkins

Angelico Press

For information, address:
Angelico Press
169 Monitor St.
Brooklyn, NY 11222
angelicopress.com
info@angelicopress.com

979-8-89280-161-4 pb
979-8-89280-162-1 cloth
979-8-89280-163-8 ebook

Cover design: Michael Schrauzer

CONTENTS

Translator's Note on the Text

WRITTEN in the seventeenth century, several versions of the text of *Le Véritable esprit des religieuses adoratrices perpétuelles du Très-Saint Sacrement de l'autel* were circulated among the houses of the Benedictines of Perpetual Adoration, sometimes handwritten and sometimes printed. I am very grateful to the community of nuns in Köln for providing me with the French edition of the text for translation. *The True Spirit* is Mother Mectilde's most important work, in which she explains the spirituality and practices of the religious Institute she founded. Mectilde was captivated by the Lamb of God, Jesus Christ, infinitely humble in the Holy Eucharist and offering Himself to the Father's glory. It is precisely in his total emptying of self, his *kenosis*, that Jesus draws the love of the Father to Himself. A share in this same life of humility and abnegation was the heart of her vision for religious who would be consecrated to the adoration—and, beyond this, imitation—of the Lord in the Blessed Sacrament. Although Mectilde's message was originally intended for religious, it expresses profound truths of benefit to every member of the Mystical Body of Christ.

Foreword

THE LIFE of Mother Mectilde[1] de Bar (1614–1698) is a wonderful testimony to the holiness of the One, Holy, Catholic
and Apostolic Church founded by Our Lord Jesus Christ.
Even relatively little-known souls such as hers illustrate the
holiness of the Church and the fact that saints, canonized and
uncanonized, well known and barely known, are manifesta-
tions of the Saint of saints, Jesus Christ himself, whose inex-
haustible person Saint John of the Cross (1542–1591) speaks
of in this way:

> Though holy doctors have uncovered many mysteries
> and wonders, and devout souls have understood them
> in this earthly condition of ours, yet the greater part still
> remains to be unfolded by them, and even to be under-
> stood by them. We must then dig deeply in Christ. He
> is like a rich mine with many pockets containing trea-
> sures: however deep we dig we will never find their end
> or their limit. Indeed, in every pocket new seams of
> fresh riches are discovered on all sides.[2]

I humbly believe that Mother Mectilde was one of those
explorers who (like that other great Benedictine mystic, Saint

---

[1] The spelling of her name confused readers for decades. Finally, it
was authoritatively established that the spelling Mectilde was the one she
herself used, and this has been adopted in all recent studies.

[2] *Spiritual Canticle*, Stanza 37:4, translation from *Liturgy of the
Hours*, vol. 4, December 14.

Gertrude of Helfta) discovered some veins of rare beauty—principally in the solemn celebration of the Divine Office, the "work of God," and then, through her hours of Eucharistic adoration—and found a way of sharing her insights and charism with her spiritual daughters and friends. The texts presented here are examples of what she discovered from living the liturgy of the Church in the context of Benedictine monastic enclosure and that of the seventeenth century, the "golden age" of French spirituality, an extraordinary era in the exploration of many rich veins of the mystery of Christ. This was the atmosphere in which Mother Mectilde lived and founded her community. While she is not regarded as one of the great lights of this period,[3] she had drunk freely at one of the great founts, Saint John Eudes (1601–1680),[4] who was a personal friend, and between them there was great mutual respect.[5] The influence of her dear friend, the layman Jean de Bernières—a very important but, at least in English, somewhat neglected figure of the French School—should also be borne in mind.

Saint John Eudes himself, in fact, is considered by many to be the best popularizer of the founder of the French school of spirituality, Cardinal Pierre de Bérulle (1575–1629),[6] by

[3] Cf. Dom Jean Leclercq, O.S.B., "A Benedictine in her century: M. Mechtilde de Bar," in Supplement to *Deus Absconditus* 71 (1980): 72–81.

[4] Cf. R. Deville, *L'école française de spiritualité* (Paris: Desclée, 1987), 81–100; William M. Thompson, ed., *Bérulle and the French School: Selected Writings* (Mahwah, NJ: Paulist Press, 1989), 291–334.

[5] Cf. Marie-Cécile Minin, mb, *Le Message marial de Catherine de Bar, Mère Mechtilde du Saint-Sacrement* (Paris: Pierre Téqui), 47–51; Paul Milcent, *Un artisan de renouveau chrétien au XVIIe siècle: Saint Jean Eudes* (Paris: Cerf, 1985), 273–78, 353, 358, 485, passim.

[6] Cf. Deville, 29–47; John Saward, *Redeemer in the Womb: Jesus Living in Mary* (San Francisco: Ignatius Press, 1993), 83–98.

whom he was formed in the spiritual life in the Oratory of France.

One of the key intuitions of the great Bérulle was his focus on what he called "the mysteries," the events in the lives of Jesus and Mary. The exterior dimension of the mystery of Jesus, for example, consists in the deeds in which he was involved on earth; these are past and unrepeatable. But the interior dimension of the mystery, which is comprised of the dispositions and inward experiences that Christ experienced during each moment of his earthly life, is eternal. In the language of Bérulle these interior dispositions of the soul of Christ are called "states." Whereas the exterior dimension of the mysteries of Christ has passed into history, the interior dimension remains forever imprinted in his soul, just as all of our experiences are imprinted in ours.

For example, Jesus was born in Bethlehem once, but that event is past; he will never be born physically as an infant again. Nonetheless all the interior dispositions or "states" of his soul at the moment of his birth and during his infancy have made a mark on his human nature. They are not transitory, but eternal; they remain in his soul. His love for the Father and total submission to him on coming into the world (cf. Heb. 10:5–7), his acceptance of complete helplessness and dependence on his Mother and his foster father, these "states" which he willingly embraced in the Incarnation, remain eternally in his soul. Even more, we can enter into these states and reproduce them in ourselves.[7] Here is the way Bérulle put it:

> The Infancy of the Son of God is but a transitory state,
> the circumstances are already past, He is a Child no

[7] See my article "The Union of the Hearts of Jesus and Mary in St. Francis de Sales and St. John Eudes," *Miles Immaculatae* 25 (1989): 488–91.

longer; yet there is something Divine in this mystery that still continues in Heaven, operating as then in a method of grace for souls on earth, whom it pleases Jesus Christ to move and consecrate to this lowly first state of His Person.[8]

So, for instance, there are souls who are particularly drawn to the mystery of Jesus' infancy like Saint Thérèse of the Child Jesus, who, so to speak appropriated the virtues of Jesus' infancy to herself by striving to reproduce these virtues in herself. This is possible, the Blessed Abbot Columba Marmion tells us, because

> These mysteries have a power that is always active and efficacious. From heaven, where He is seated at the right hand of God His Father, Christ continues to communicate to souls the fruits of His states, so as to effect in those souls their divine resemblance to Him.[9]

Thus, we find this beautiful text in a chapter address given by Mother Mectilde on December 17, 1671:

> It is true that the mystery is past, I recognize it, and that it happened only once, but the grace of the mystery is not, in fact, past for the souls who prepare themselves to give birth to Jesus Christ in their heart. He was born one time in Bethlehem, and He is born every day in us with Holy Communion, which, as the Fathers say, is an extension of the Incarnation.
>
> Do you know why Our Lord did not want to be born in the city of Jerusalem? It is because in that city, all was full of creatures; there was not a single empty house. All

---

[8] Cited in Henri Bremond, *A Literary History of Religious Thought in France III: The Triumph of Mysticism* (London: S.P.C.K., 1936), 59–60.

[9] Blessed Columba Marmion, O.S.B., *Christ in His Mysteries*, trans. Alan Bancroft (Bethesda, MD: Zaccheus Press, 2008), 23.

was full of business or something other. He preferred to be born in a poor stable, empty and abandoned. This demonstrates to us that, if we want Jesus to abide in us, we must empty ourselves of all things, without exception. This being done, He will impress in us His spirit, His life, His inclinations, and in such a soul one will see only Jesus. Those who have received this grace will be recognized easily by their docility and simplicity, the companion virtues of holy childhood.

Who are the first to come to the Infant Jesus to offer Him homage? Poor folk, shepherds. It is what the Gospel says: "Ye who are little, come unto Me." Only the humble are worthy of learning secrets so divine, hidden from the great ones of the earth, who are precisely the proud. The more a soul is little, the more will God communicate Himself to her. He goes to seek her out in the depth of her nothingness, where He fills her with all Himself.

Now let us note how Saint John Eudes applied this doctrine in his teaching, beautifully embodied in his treatise entitled *The Kingdom of Jesus*:

You cannot too often realize and reflect on the truth that the mysteries of the life of Christ have not yet reached their full perfection and completeness. Although they are perfect and complete in Christ's own Person, they are not yet completed in you who are His members, nor in Holy Mother Church, which is His Mystical Body. It is the plan of the Son of God that His whole Church should participate in and actually be, as it were, the continuation and extension of the mystery of His Incarnation, birth, childhood, hidden life, public life of teaching and of labor, His Passion and His death, by the graces He desires to impart to you, and by the effects He wishes to accomplish in you through these same mysteries. By this means, He desires to fulfill His mysteries in you. . . .

So, the Son of God plans to perfect and complete in you all His states and mysteries. He intends to fulfill in you the divine life which has been His for all eternity in the bosom of His Father, imparting a participation in that life, and making you live, with Him, a life entirely pure and holy.[10]

We will note that when Mother Mectilde uses the word "state" it is virtually always with reference to the state of victimhood, which she wishes her sisters to live, especially in adoration and reparation before the Most Blessed Sacrament. When she uses the term "mystery" it is virtually always with reference to Jesus's presence in the Eucharist. These are key words in terms of defining the Benedictine family to which she gave birth. We will also note that Mectilde very frequently spoke of being in the "state of the host," particularly in chapter XVIII, exhorting her nuns to place themselves in the same state as that in which Jesus abides in the sacred Host, proposing this as a kind of template of her unique form of Benedictine life. She also finds in the death of the great Patriarch of Western Monasticism a model of the life she proposes: one that conforms to the holy death of Benedict in the oratory before the Blessed Sacrament (see chapter XX).

In this connection, modern readers of *The True Spirit* must bear in mind that it was indeed a handbook for nuns, for women discerning this radical charism of a life devoted entirely to a silent and perpetual adoration in reparation for

---

[10] Saint John Eudes, *The Kingdom of Jesus in Christian Souls: A Treatise on Christian Perfection for Use by Clergy or Laity*, trans. a Trappist Father (New York: P. J. Kenedy & Sons, 1946), 251–52.

sinners. This little work was not intended for just any casual reader, and that remains true: only those who are hungering and thirsting for the kingdom of God, and are ready to embrace the hard ways by which God may lead them closer to Himself in solidarity with Christ on the Cross, are ready for Mother Mectilde's teaching. It is not for nothing that she has been compared, by scholars, to St. John of the Cross, with whose writings she was well acquainted. Some of Mother Mectilde's language will sound extreme in this day and age. She is, in fact, teaching the Gospel message in all its radicalness, but with the hyperbole characteristic of *le grand siècle*, the seventeenth century in France. The hyperbole is in service of conveying the radicalness, and in this regard we moderns, too, can receive it as a wake-up call.

Another very significant factor to note is that Pope Pius XI at the time of the beatification of John Eudes in 1925 described him as "father, doctor, and apostle of the cultus of the Hearts of Jesus and Mary"[11] whose Hearts he had striven all his life to glorify with liturgical feasts and in his *magnum opus*, *The Admirable Heart of Mary*,[12] as well as in his other works. Mother Mectilde would certainly have been familiar with his theology of the Hearts of Jesus and Mary and, indeed, we find her speaking frequently in these chapter addresses about the Heart of Jesus, a theology subsequently embraced in the bosom of the Church, which was emerging

[11] *Acta Apostolicæ Sedis* 17 (1925): 482–97.

[12] Saint John Eudes finished writing *Le Cœur Admirable de la Très Sacrée Mère de Dieu* shortly before his death. Major sections of this huge work appear in Saint John Eudes, *The Admirable Heart of Mary*, trans. Charles di Targiani and Ruth Hauser (New York: P.J. Kenedy & Sons, 1948) and Saint John Eudes, *The Sacred Heart of Jesus*, trans. Dom Richard Flower, O.S.B. (New York: P.J. Kenedy & Sons, 1946). The work has never been rendered into English in its entirety.

from the French school of spirituality even before the revelations of Paray-le-Monial became known. In a marginal comment the great Jesuit scholar of the Most Sacred of Jesus, Édouard Glotin, observes that "with Mectilde and Margaret-Mary one oscillates between reparative adoration and self-offering in the state of victimhood."[13]

My hope is that these considerations will provide valuable context for the rich spiritual teaching of Mother Mectilde of the Most Blessed Sacrament.

† Msgr. ARTHUR BURTON CALKINS[14]

---

[13] Édouard Glotin, S.J., *La Bible du Cœur de Jésus: Un Livre de Vie pour le générations du IIIe millenaire* (Paris: Presses de la Renaissance, 2007), 337.

[14] Msgr. Calkins submitted this Foreword on December 22, 2023. This would have been on of the last things he wrote before he died on February 3, 2024. *Requiescat in pace.*

The True Spirit
of the Perpetual Adorers
of the Most Holy Sacrament
of the Altar

I

Counsels and rules for the
Daughters of the Most Holy Sacrament

SINCE GOD has made this Institute for the glory of His Son, in the infinite humiliations He bears in the divine Eucharist, the souls who are called to it must live there in an angelic purity, through complete detachment from themselves.

When a girl enters religious life, she may be doing so for the motive of saving her soul and gaining eternal beatitude. However, in the Institute of the Most Holy Sacrament, we should have no other intention than the pure glory of this Mystery; this is why the religious of the Most Holy Sacrament are called its victims. The reason for this is easy to understand, since they have no other motive in their whole life than to honor God immolated and continually annihilated under the species of bread and wine. They are victims of the Sacramental Jesus,[1] so that, in offering themselves, they render an infinite homage (if such a thing were possible) to the sacramental Existence of Jesus, who is every day destroyed in our bosoms, to the glory of His Father. Every created thing is corrupted and destroyed by the passage of time, confessing by its destruction that God alone exists through Himself. But in the Blessed Sacrament, Jesus Christ annihilates Himself every day, to confess and exalt the infinite Being of His Father; and few souls apply themselves to adoration of this infinite humility. Not only does He exhaust His sacramental Being in reverence and homage to God His Father, but He does it in the most humiliating way He could choose, which far surpasses the humiliations of

---

[1] Literally, Jesus-made-sacrament.

the Cross, since there He was nailed to the wood (which itself had no ill will toward Jesus Christ). However, in the Most Holy Sacrament of the Altar, He descends into hearts abominable and corrupted by the infection of sin; and often He dwells in places more infamous than we can conceive, for which He has an intense horror. Yes, He descends there, and makes His abode there as long as the sacramental Species lasts in those detestable stomachs. Oh! If we could comprehend the purity and holiness of Jesus Christ, we would have some idea of the profound humiliation which He has in the hearts of the impious, and those who are so abominable that they receive Communion unworthily. This is the first step of Jesus in this mystery. Let us pass on to others in attentive reflection: they are more easily understood and touch the feelings more, but we should acknowledge that this first point is the most terrible for Jesus Christ.

Let us consider the profanations which the godless and sorcerers make of those precious and adorable Hosts. We should die simply remembering such things. And without a miracle, there are some souls who would not be able to bear the abominable evils which these devils incarnate do to our divine Savior Jesus Christ. We should pass over these evils in silence since we cannot speak forcefully enough about them; but the truth is, we ought to die of sorrow at seeing the infinite love of God so unworthily repaid. Yes, I can say it, and I wish my heart would break in saying it, that, in return for the incomprehensible charity of Jesus Christ and His passionate love for mankind, the wicked wrench Him from His Eucharistic throne and they do things of which one dare not speak. But with such rage as surpasses that of the demons, they throw themselves on the divine Hosts with an inexplicable insatiability to destroy Jesus Christ, and subdue Him by shameful treatment which cannot be named, which we might call infinite in some way, on account of the violence of their malice. No more than this is needed to give the death blow to a heart who loves Jesus Christ; this should at least wound it in such a way as never to be healed.

But how many other outrages could we recount? Let us leave such things to the solicitude of love which will investigate them better than we. Next, let us say, given all Our Lord suffers in the Holy Eucharist, is it not right that there are some souls who, by the powerful impulse of love and reverence for a Majesty so profaned, vow and consecrate themselves to this divine Mystery, in the spirit of victims, in order to suffer (if it were possible) all that Jesus suffers, to be able to defend Him from these mortal wounds and preserve Him from these horrible humiliations? Can we find it strange that the Spirit of God inspired the building of monasteries where souls are received for this purpose, and without any other consideration than the glory of Jesus in the Eucharist? So that, as much as they can, they gather in their hearts all the gratitude sinners should render to Jesus Christ in return for the excess of His love; and that these souls should ceaselessly be sacrificed to God's justice for blasphemers, as much to repair the glory and honor stolen from Jesus Christ their adorable Savior, as to obtain mercy for sinners and the grace to do penance for their crimes!

Would anyone wish to extinguish one tiny spark of the charity of Jesus Christ burning in the hearts of these victims, who produce, by their reverence and their resemblance to the Savior, the two effects which came through His death, namely, to satisfy the justice of His Father by repairing His glory, and to effect the salvation of the world? Here is the task of this little group, although we are infinitely incapable of succeeding in it, except in union with Jesus Christ, from whom we draw the merit and life of all our actions.

Here are the obligation of the Daughters of the Blessed Sacrament and the purpose of their vocation; and if someone does not have this intention in her soul, she should not claim the title of victim of the Most Blessed Sacrament.

Do we understand from the little we have just said, what the object and aim of our holy Institute is, and why God has established it? It is our first obligation to fully understand the principle and the intention of Jesus Christ in founding it. Therefore, we must help souls to understand this who aspire to it and who desire to enter; they must know what God expects of them, and whether they are sufficiently generous to embrace it.

Many will not comprehend anything at first about what it is to be a victim; also it will not be easy to understand for the souls who still have not tasted the ways and guidance of grace. Nevertheless, it is absolutely necessary that they know, from the start, what they intend to engage in, supposing that God chooses them to have this state. For He receives with love those who would vow themselves to His service as victims, but very few are capable of enduring the consequences. It is not necessary to descend to particulars about these prodigious actions; it is not even relevant to explain them. The souls whom God will honor in associating them by state with His Son, victim of God's justice and holiness for sin, will experience things which are beyond words. Although this state is rigorous, it is sustained by a divine grace; still, this remains unknown to the soul possessing it. It is not an ordinary state, but only for those favored persons in whom God takes delight insofar as they are in His Son, if one may speak this way. Let us pass over these, then, to enjoy their felicity, and say a word about the ordinary states we should have, or at least try to acquire with all our strength.

First, you will observe that no one can be a Religious of the

Institute for the sake of self-interest or for any return to one-self, and that this would be a failure of the purity of intention with which one should offer oneself as a victim. A Daughter of the Most Holy Sacrament must be detached from herself, from the world, and from all that nature seeks of grandeur and pleasure. For those who are not sufficiently instructed about the spirit of this Institute, they must be given a brief lesson on it during the time they are postulants, so that having understood its purity and excellence they may ask for this grace from Jesus Christ with all humility and fervor. This purity of intention is the chief ornament of a Daughter of the Blessed Sacrament and she should be adorned with it in order to present herself before her God, her King, and her Sovereign. She must intend nothing else than to come to be sacrificed to God, but it must be in a complete way and not by halves. She must give herself to Him with all the capacity of her being, at least with all her will, awaiting the light of the divine Sun which will illuminate the depths of her soul to teach her in what way she should give herself to Jesus Christ.

In the second place, after she has considered God according to the purity of His good pleasure and the order of His divine will, she should resolve to live henceforth for Him alone. And what will be her life in such a holy place? It is a life which should be called a perpetual death, since her obligation requires her to separate herself continually from creatures and from self, taking for her model Jesus Christ's example in the adorable Eucharist from the first moment. She must study and observe so exactly the states and dispositions He has there that there is not a single moment of her life in which she does not honor one of them, either through likeness or by tending toward it through love and union. We have said elsewhere how souls called to this holy Institute must have, as much as possible, this precious resemblance to their God and their

Spouse Jesus Christ in this divine Sacrament. We must still explain what it means practically to be a victim, and in what this perpetual immolation consists, which the Daughters of the Holy Sacrament are obligated to every day, so that they may imitate, according to their ability, Jesus Christ ceaselessly immolated to His Father.

My Sisters, this continual sacrifice requires two things. First, a pure gaze upon God, just as Jesus eternally beholds His Father. Second, self-forgetfulness, by a holy neglect of the infinity of things with which we are busy in various ways; first, by affection or desire, etc., then by fear of some humiliation or anxiety, or the privation of some pleasure; now in considering the actions of others, and the thousand similar things which sometimes keep us so occupied and so attached to them that we lose our interior attention to God. This wretched inclination which we have toward ourselves has such malignity that it makes us incapable of beholding God and resembling Jesus in the Host. We should not distance ourselves from our adorable object; since He is our divine model, we should have Him always before our eyes. We should do always what He Himself does, because we should follow in His footsteps.

This is not an idle fancy or a fantastical position based on an unreasonable idea. It is the obligation of all Christians to imitate Jesus, but especially a Daughter of the Most Holy Sacrament must imitate Jesus as much as she can. Continue, then, to contemplate what Jesus Christ does in this august Sacrament; see how He has no other object than the glory of His Father, as if He forgets His own interests. This is proved by the fact that He is handed over to the wicked and even to animals, and by the fact that He is often kept in churches which are totally unworthy, if not insulting. Alas! All alone, without a visitor, or only rarely, and all the other things we have already discussed. Thus you see that He does not consider Himself at all, and that He is a victim in this mystery. There Jesus is offered to His Father, and in each soul who receives Him in Holy Communion, to render to the divine Majesty the infinite homage and adoration owed to Him, since the soul is incapable of doing this because of its unworthiness and its very limited abilities.

Yes, my Sisters, this is wonderful. Jesus Christ enters our hearts in order to celebrate there a divine and eternal sacrifice, infinite in merit. This should give us a great love for Holy Communion, since Jesus Christ performs in us the office of High Priest and sovereign Sacrificer, by immolating Himself for the soul who receives Him and because His divine sacrifice gives an infinite homage and glory to God His Father.

We could write a whole volume on this precious and most noble subject, for it seems to me so important to encourage timid souls to receive Holy Communion and to teach them the simple and very easy way to comport themselves therein. However, let us leave that discussion in order to show the two continual activities of Jesus in the Host. The first is His eternal gaze towards God His Father, which we just mentioned. The second concerns the salvation of mankind and also constitutes the second goal of our vocation in the Institute, namely, zeal for the conversion of sinners, and primarily for those who desecrate this august Mystery.

Sisters, could you have more noble aims than those which Jesus had? He had only these two goals before His eyes, at every moment of His life. A soul who has no others is truly detached from herself, and if she perseveres, will undoubtedly become a very faithful copy of that divine original.

I am not wandering from my subject, though I am interrupting a bit; let us conclude by saying that if we could have asked the ancient sacrificial victim (had it been rational) the reason for all its actions, for example, why it took nourishment, and so on, it would have responded that, as victim, it was destined for sacrifice and consequently, it lived only to die; and that it longed for death continually. Why death? "In order to confess by my destruction," it would say, "the infinite sovereignty of the divine Being." And this is what Jesus does in the Host, and what we should do in imitation of Him. This is His state and His disposition towards the supreme Majesty and infinite Being of God His Father.

He gives glory to God His Father in the Most Holy Sacrament in two ways. First, by the homage which He gives to Him through the infinite abasement of His divine Person. Second, by making Himself a slave for sinners (if one may use such a term, yes, with all reverence), because there He becomes the ransom and pledge which satisfies divine justice in all its rigor. In the first, He annihilates Himself infinitely in homage to the divine Grandeur. Through the second, He humbles Himself as if by a double annihilation, taking on Himself all the wretchedness of mankind; and, to put it in one word, taking on Himself our sins, becoming a criminal, and bearing (without any exception) all that sin merits of sorrow, humiliation, and so on.

The first humiliation of Jesus is infinite in excellence. The second, which cannot be expressed, casts souls into a profound astonishment, making them say, with St. John, "God so loved the world that He gave His only Son,"[2] not only as its liberator, but also as its slave, because He was reduced to bearing the awful weight of sin. By this burden He became the prey of divine justice, so that it was fully satisfied by Him, because He had an infinite capacity for bearing it. Oh! If only we could understand how abominable sin is! It must be truly

---

[2] John 3:16.

terrible since it required a God to be annihilated in order to destroy it and to merit for us the grace which we had lost, so as to enter again into God's friendship. It was to accomplish this that He came to earth and He continues to do this in the Most Holy Eucharist. There He is adoring, loving, and exalting God His Father. But we must add that in the Eucharist He is suffering: there He is scorned, forgotten by the majority of men, He is desecrated, and too often handed over to the power of His enemies who treat Him in this Mystery in a way which one would not dare to describe. Nevertheless He says not a word; He does not complain, even though He suffers indignities from sinners and the abominations of the impious. And why? Because He is there as a victim. [In the Holy Eucharist,] Jesus is dead and dies every day through the continuation of His divine sacrifice.[3]

This is the state which we also should bear, by abasing ourselves completely before the infinite majesty of God, by a double annihilation of humiliation, shame, and embarrassment for our sins and for those of our brethren. This last point burdens us with every kind of sorrow and shame, and all that sin merits. You see, then, to what destruction we should be reduced? We cannot express the kind of loss of self we should bear and the sort of rejection to be endured from God's side. For, being sinners, charged with our own crimes and with those of other sinners, should we expect pleasant treatment? Oh! Without doubt, we would be mistaken if we expected to find, bearing the title of victim, the delights of the interior life and if, having the rope around the neck and taken the torch in hand, we thought we would be well received at the table of the Lord and partake of the favors of His love.

---

[3] The thinkers of the French School held that in the Eucharist all the mysteries of Jesus Christ's life perdure. See the Foreword to this volume.

Another error is to imagine yourself as lacking the right dispositions if you are deprived of the consolations and lights often deemed necessary to be in God's favor and so that you may be sure your devotion is pleasing to God or at least that you are not condemned. Oh! You are mistaken—for you have resolved to be a victim, and have placed the rope around your neck—if you do not expect from God lightning, thunder, storms and harsh treatment. You are criminals, my dear Sisters! In yourself and in your brethren. You are sacrificed in order to destroy sin and to repair, if possible, the glory it steals from God. You do what Jesus did, although in a very unequal way. Therefore, you must resolve to be treated like Him, not on the order of the infinite, of which you are not capable, but according to God's order, and to the degree it pleases Him for you to satisfy His justice.

This is what we must endure; to explain this would be very difficult, because we should envision it as being as many different states as there are souls consecrated to it, since each state has particular effects. And while it is true that in the houses of the Most Holy Sacrament all the Religious are consecrated as victims, nevertheless, each only has a resemblance of state, since each soul has the part which Jesus gives to her. This is done according to the divine wisdom which knows and is aware of the strength of each one He has destined from all eternity to have a small share in these sacred and sorrowful states. It is the same in the Holy Eucharist, continually applied to souls who are consecrated to Him to merit grace, to enter into and to endure these states. Oh! If we knew the secret ways of God in leading souls, we would be careful to keep from complaining, from murmuring, from becoming anxious about the arrangement of troubles, sufferings, temptations, and humiliations; if we had a little faith and patience, we would discover infinite marvels which I could call mysteries.

10

To explain a little more fully, it would require as many treatises as there are actions [in souls], so true is it that each is different and that in each one Jesus Christ is adored and bears these states in an infinite way, but all are sanctifying, although very humiliating. It is not fitting for me to say much more, just as the blind should not speak about the light, for they know nothing about it; just so, someone who has no point of entry or share of the life of Jesus Christ should not speak about His suffering, sanctifying love and His rejoicing in souls.

Sisters, when I consider the infinite happiness of the Daughters of the Blessed Sacrament, I am beside myself: for the more I consider this undertaking, though very small in the eyes of men, the greater I find it in God's light. Do not think I am exaggerating. No, no, I can say it with all sincerity, all the greatness of this work draws its value and excellence from Jesus annihilated in the Host. It is a product of His love, an emanation from the state He has there. It ought to produce wonderful effects in our hearts, but we are not aware of this, since we fail to give ourselves to the Eucharistic mystery in the purity of holy detachment. Oh! What marvelous things Jesus intends to do in the souls whom He has chosen as victims! One of the most surprising, my Sisters, is to communicate to us His Eucharistic life. What is this life? He is in the Eucharist to be eaten by us, in order to nourish us, to sustain us with Himself; and His intention is to have His fill of us for His delight. But how can He be fed? By eating, my Sisters. He consumes us and being in our breast, we are in His Heart; He lives in us according to the life we give Him; since, just as we put Him to death by sin, likewise, we give Him life by our fidelity. We know by experience that He lives admirably in some persons and that He languishes in others, according to the different states and dispositions of souls. Therefore, our care and vigilance, our love and fidelity give Him life more or less vigorously. It is in our power, my Sisters, to make Jesus live in us through His grace.

However, there is yet another sort of life He lives in His dear friends. And I fervently wish He lived this life in us, because this life of His is infinitely glorious and He receives more glory from one soul in whom He lives that life than from whole kingdoms where such souls are not found. What is this precious life? I cannot express it, Sisters. The Fathers, saying what they would, depicted the very intimate union God has with us in the Holy Eucharist, but the nature and effects of this life are indescribable. I can say this without exaggerating or fearing the imagination's weakness. My Sisters, it is through this life, without my being able to express it further, that Jesus my Savior desires to live in us. I know it is the result of His divine power and that the servants of God regard it as miraculous when they find it in someone. However, this miracle is not rare because of Jesus, since it is His intention and the only reason for which He instituted His august Sacrament; rather, the wonder of the great men is at finding so few souls on earth who resolve to become capable of receiving it in all its fullness.

II

The dispositions Daughters should have when entering monasteries of the Institute

WHEN A DAUGHTER leaves the world, she should apply to herself the words which Our Lord spoke to the one whom He called to follow Him, "Leave the dead to bury the dead."[4] She should enter the cloister in a spirit of separation and, having done so, she should not allow her mind to return to the world, or waste time thinking about what she has left, in order to give herself to the One who did her the honor of choosing her. It happens often too, that she separates herself courageously from all those she loves most dearly, but the devil, envious of her good, tries to blunt the point of her fervor and to overcome it. To succeed in this, he represents to her that she left the sweetness of her freedom and even the good she could do in the world. Thus, little by little, she allows herself to be preoccupied by the idea of return and thinking about the "flesh pots of Egypt,"[5] and she falls into an apathy which gives her distaste for her undertaking and imperceptibly removes from her the courage with which she gave herself to the sacrifice of holy Religion. She should enter there as if into a holy desert, locking herself away with the Son of God in the Holy Eucharist, where she should not look for any company other than His holy Presence. Since she enters only for Him, she should learn to be content with Him

[4] Luke 9:60; Matthew 8:22.
[5] Cf. Exodus 16:3.

13

alone. It would be an intolerable insult to share her affection with creatures; it would be saying to Him that His love and His infinite perfections are not enough to fill the capacity of her heart. For this reason we exhort the Daughters who enter the cloister never voluntarily to return in thought to the family home or think of anything which they have left behind in order to give themselves to Jesus Christ.

On coming into the monastery, after having purified the heart by sprinkling with holy water, which shows that nothing impure should come into the holy place, we then present the crucifix to the Daughter to show her that she comes in order to embrace the crucified life, and that she should begin a new life in Jesus Christ. She is brought to the Church so that she might kneel before the majesty of God hidden in the Divine Sacrament of the altar, where she should offer her heart to be sacrificed to the glory of this Holy God, who receives her in His infinite kindness. From this moment, she should try to remain in that precious solitude, by being separated completely from the world and herself, to live for Jesus Christ alone.

To my thinking, a soul detached in this way is a marvel, a miracle of grace and a masterpiece from the omnipotent hand of God. Why? Because we hold on to ourselves so tightly that there is almost no one generous enough to cleave to God's designs, to renounce self and be crucified to this extent. Let us weep, my Sisters, let us weep for this great evil. Let us weep to see the divine life neglected in the adorable Eucharist. Let us weep because our divine Savior can find no one who wants to be detached as they must in order to receive it. But let us also weep for ourselves, since being the children and heirs of this divine life we do not put ourselves in the state to give Him the joy of producing it in us. Oh! If we could understand its dignity and excellence! We would die of regret at not having focused our care and actions on this infinite good! I seem to hear the adorable voice of that divine prisoner of love, who calls to us from the depths of the tabernacle, "My children, it is to you that I should leave My treasures as an inheritance. It is for you, who are consecrated to My love, to share the interests of My glory, to have as your portion the shame and contempt which I receive. You give yourselves to Me by the sacrifice of your lives; I want to give Myself to you to make you live with My entirely divine life."

Yes, my Sisters, it seems to me that Our Lord desires, even in this present life, to reward us for the very slight sacrifice we make of our lives in honor of His divine Sacrament. He does us the favor of admitting us to His table, and I add, into His paternal bosom. He wants us to have no other treasure than Himself. Oh! Too greedy is the person for whom Jesus in the Holy Eucharist is not enough! My Sisters, if I asked you if you want any other treasures, you would answer me heartily that you despise all other things, and that eating the flesh of the God Man, you have no fear of dying of hunger.

My Sisters, let us eat this adorable bread, for this is bread which contains life in itself. However, the one who eats only to sustain life does not look for the pleasure of taste in eating: I do not say that you cannot taste this divine bread, since it has a heavenly taste and savor; but do not taste it with your senses, they cannot receive the delicacy of this wonderful taste. Savor it with a pure and naked faith and you will experience that it has the taste of the living God. Eating in this way, you will have life in you.

Learn to please Him; drive out creatures from your hearts, for you are the chosen Daughters of the immolated God, and He causes you to enter into His divine Sacrifice. Your glory and your privilege are to belong to Him, to share with Him all the shame, all the humiliations which He suffers in this pre-

15

cious mystery. If He dwells there hidden and unknown by men, He wants your faith to discover Him there, He wants you to enter into participation in the states He has. Alas! My Sisters, is your heart not pierced by a thousand sorrows when you see your admirable Host dwelling among sinners and those who profane His glory? He is insulted by the wicked, despised, neglected and almost unknown among men; and finally, so few persons adore Him and believe that He is truly present in this divine Sacrament that faith seems nearly dead in their hearts—at least, we see very few who are animated by it. Nevertheless, Jesus, God and Man, is day and night in this ineffable Sacrament. But *for whom*, my Sisters, if not *for you*, so that you go in search of Him, to give Him your worship and adoration unceasingly? It is for you that He is in the Tabernacle, and I say truthfully, more for you than for anyone, since He has made this Institute to receive you there and He wants to be the object of your perpetual adoration. And maybe, my Sisters, none of you would have been a Religious if you were not a Daughter of the Holy Sacrament. Oh, my Sisters, how great is this grace! How elevated it is! And to what a high level of sanctity it brings a soul! Can you ever esteem it highly enough? But we say its worth is infinite. Beware of neglecting it; happy is the soul which understands its excellence and receives it with the love, zeal, and fidelity she should! You are, my Sisters, the Daughters of this divine mystery.

Now, if you are the Daughters, where are your connections with your Father? Where are your belongings, your dependencies, and your relations? A child has everything from his father: his habits, his inclinations, and all the rest. See if you find these things in yourself. What are the inclinations of Jesus? Oh, Sisters, you know: an ardent thirst for contempt, for poverty, and for suffering. This is what speaks most clearly in His holy life and in the adorable mystery of His love. Alas!

16

What contempt, what poverty, what sorrow! For, although in one way He is impassible, in another, does He not suffer frightful treatment from sinners and blasphemers? As for poverty and contempt, there is no need to say more, it is obvious. We say only, Sisters, that our principal task is to bind ourselves to Him and to have a resemblance to Him in the Eucharist; and without this connection to His life of abjection and suffering it is impossible for us to be victims of His justice for those who profane the Eucharist.

Therefore, the delights of a Daughter of the Blessed Sacrament are, first, to be unknown.

Second, she should not hold any position or occupy any rank, that is, she should be forgotten by everyone if possible, or at least have a fervent desire for this.

Third, she should think always that she deserves the last place, and if obedience jeopardizes that [e.g., becoming a superior], she should show that she always remains in spirit beneath everyone, never losing the sense of her abjection.

Fourth, she should do good to everyone without the hope of gratitude.

Fifth, she should be poor in esteem, honor, and affection from creatures.

Sixth, it should be a joy to her to be without talent and destitute of anything which could cause her to be noticed.

Seventh, she should love solitude and remain hidden like the Son of God in the Tabernacle, never willingly admitting any creature into her heart, but keeping it detached from all that would hinder it from being like the sacred ciborium which contains only Jesus Christ.

Eighth, she should be continually in a love of abandonment for the sake of sinners, offering her life to God at every moment for their complete conversion, through a sincere return to grace.

Ninth, she should be insatiable for scorn and contempt, not thinking herself a true daughter of the Blessed Sacrament unless she has the honor of being heaped with them.

Tenth, she should receive suffering in the same way as contempt, both the one and the other being a portion and gift from Jesus Christ, when it pleases Him to provide occasions for them; she should welcome these with as much respect, veneration, and submission as she would the divine Savior in Holy Communion. This will surprise you, my Sisters, but I know what I am saying about this, and what a mystery of grace is hidden in contempt. Ah! If we understood it, everyone would come to love it to excess! But these are Jesus' secrets which are only discovered by His closest friends.

Carry out these things, my Sisters, with courage, fidelity, and perseverance and you will soon be capable of receiving Jesus' divine life, which He so desires to give us and make us live, just as He lives it Himself. You will preserve this life in yourselves if you avoid falling into certain weaknesses which seem to be rather common among souls who are not yet steady in the solid practice of holy annihilation. Meanwhile we must avoid them as much as possible. We will point out several.

First, never oppose anyone, argue, or insist on your opinion.

Second, never prefer yourself to anyone else but believe yourself lower than the worst sinners.

Third, never look for esteem or honor from any creature.

Fourth, do not admit any affection into your heart which could separate you from grace even for a moment; there are affections which join us to Jesus Christ, and these are not prejudicial to it. But do not be led astray, my Sisters: you will know your friendship is holy when it keeps you united to God and if it produces neither disturbance nor any other bad effect in your interior.

Fifth, never reject or despise anyone.

Sixth, love dearly the weak and sinners, because they are doubly precious to Jesus Christ.

Seventh, love your neighbor and especially your Sisters with a tender love, thus following the commandment of Jesus, that you love one another with the same love with which He loves you. You ought to love in this way so that His prayer may be effective in you, "That they may be one, Father, as You and I are one."[6] Alas! who would be so wretched as to be opposed to the effects of this divine prayer? It is God who prays to God; finally, those are the desires of the adorable Heart of Jesus Christ. It is for you, my Sisters, as His beloved daughters, to fulfill them faithfully.

[6] John 17:22.

19

III

The three dwellings of God

THE ROYAL PROPHET speaks these words in the form of a prayer: "*Unam petii a Domino, hanc requiram ... etc.*"[7] My God, I ask you for the grace to remain all the days of my life in Your house. In another place, the same Prophet says again: "*Beati qui habitant in domo tua Domine, etc.*"[8] Blessed are those who dwell in your house, O Lord, they will praise and glorify You forever. And elsewhere it is said, "*Laetatus sum in his quae dicta sunt mihi, in domum, etc.*"[9] I rejoiced when they said to me, let us go into the house of the Lord. What does the holy king mean by this joy and beatitude, unless he intends to speak of the house of glory, where there is only joy, delight, splendor and perfect peace!

My Sisters, you know that there are three houses of God, which we may call mansions and dwellings. The first is the celestial dwelling which we call the heavenly empyrean, which God inhabits in His grandeur and magnificence, where His infinite perfections shine with an indescribable glory and excellence, and are beyond the understanding of our minds. This is the place where He fills the blessed with His glorious presence; there is never darkness, pain, or want there, but a perfect fullness of eternal felicity.

The second house of God is the Church, where God abides in a corporeal manner, in the august Sacrament of the altar,

[7] Psalm 27:4.
[8] Psalm 83:4.
[9] Psalm 121:1.

where we should go to adore Him. It is of this holy house that the Prophet said: *"Elegi abjectus esse in domo Domini,* etc."[10] I have chosen to be little and abject in the house of the Lord, rather than to be great in the palaces of kings and in the dwelling of sinners.

My Sisters, we can say you are in this second house, since having the glory to be Christians and Religious, you live in the house of God and in the palace of the Lord. Oh! What happiness to live with God, in the house of God Himself! My Sisters, if someone asks you where you live, with whom you dwell, say, "I dwell in God's house. I live with God Himself! I take my meals with Him, I sit at His table, close to Him, and I am fed with His very Self." How wonderful and rapturous it is! Oh! If we understand our happiness and the good fortune we have, we would have a marvelous appreciation for the favor God is granting us. We admire it when a king invites an inferior to eat at his table. We regard a person most fortunate when the king has him live in his palace; and when, as a sign of his affection, keeps the person whom he favors close to his majesty; everyone seems to envy the honor the king shows him. Oh! What are all the flatteries of earthly monarchs compared with the smallest favor God grants us, keeping us so close to His infinite grandeur, vivifying us with His presence and His love! But in Christianity and even in monasteries, not all the Christians and the Religious are sanctified; and though they dwell in the temporal house of God, they sometimes continue in their infidelities and fall into divine disgrace. (We know through our experience that we are not perfect, though we live in the cloister, which is the house of God.)

We should speak next of God's third dwelling, which is in our souls. In that palace He resides with immense delight. In

---

[10] Psalm 83:10.

the dwelling of a pure soul He communicates Himself to her fully and He restores His image in her, which sin effaced. This is the precious house which is spoken of in the Gospel under many figures: as a treasure hidden in a field, a precious pearl, the leaven hidden in the mass of flour, and so on. This is the place where the Prophet asked to dwell all the days of his life, knowing that he could not go to heaven, into the house of glory, without dying and consequently without ending and finishing his days. You see, therefore, that he humbly asked God to remain always in His house which is the depth of his soul, where God truly dwells. The three divine Persons are in the soul as in their temple. They carry out the operations of their divine love there; in this place the soul receives the likeness [to God] she lost through sin.

Sisters, sin cannot completely remove from us the image and character of God; but it does completely remove the likeness which we were given in baptism and which Adam received at the beginning of his creation, when God said, "Let us make man in our image and likeness."[11] But in that hidden place the soul is restored to a wholly divine beauty and is rendered like God through Jesus Christ. Through Him everything is repaired in the soul and she enters again into all the perfections which she had lost.

My Sisters, we should try to establish our dwelling in this interior mansion. To succeed in this we must be despoiled in several ways at the foot of the Cross. We must be stripped like the good thief, to whom Our Lord promised entry into Paradise with Himself. Faith is required to enter into it, faith is required to stay in it, and faith and love are both required to be perfected in it. The beginning of this entry is harsh and difficult, and the soul feels great repugnance. However, what fol-

[11] Genesis 1:26.

lows becomes delightful. At the start everything seems dark, narrow and as if inaccessible; but a little courage, patience, and fidelity lead us into it.

Each person should observe the movements of her soul to perceive the hidden path along which God desires the soul to walk to perfection. It is essential to know how she ought to proceed. With a holy confidence, you should often say this verse of the Prophet, "*Vias tuas, Domine, demonstra mihi.*"[12] Show me Thy ways, O Lord, and teach me the hidden path in which I should walk to be united to Thee. This path is in some way hidden from our senses, which always want to see, know, taste, and feel. It is narrow; that is why to walk in it we have to be stripped of our own understanding and affections. Faith alone should be our guide, and we need no other light or support.

Therefore, since it is impossible to dwell in the blessed house of our interior without being stripped, let us strive diligently to be detached from ourselves, as this is what hinders us the most. Oh, what sorrow at death to see that we have had in our soul's mansion the entire Most Holy Trinity; that we had God Himself in our possession for so many years, without rejoicing in His presence, without believing it, or discerning it. Worldly people, who are ignorant of such marvelous truths, may hope to find some excuse. But we, my Sisters, who have been taught and told it every day, what will we say? As for me, I think that this will be the soul's most cruel grief, to see what she lost through her own fault, to understand what she possessed without profit, to know that all of Paradise dwelt in her, and she remained in a wretched imprisonment to creatures and self. See then, my Sisters, that this is

---

[12] Psalm 24:4.

the house God desires to dwell in and that He also desires you to dwell with Him.

The first dwelling (I mean heaven) is only given to those who have spent their life in the other two. In the second house, few become saints, and it is difficult to be perfect there because of dealings with sinners, who exist also in the Catholic Church, like the weeds among the good grain; unless one enters and dwells in this third mansion of the Lord, where one is brought to the delights of the first [dwelling]. Some holy martyrs who knew God in a moment, and who confessed Him immediately having received the grace of martyrdom, entered into celestial beatitude, having only fleetingly remained in the abode of their interior. But we, who cannot be martyrs now by the shedding of our blood, should enter into the mansion of our soul in order to be purified and go to Jesus Christ.

My Sisters, this is the beatitude of the saints while on earth. Moreover, a servant of God said she was no longer troubled by anything since she found in her heart the same Paradise which the saints possess in glory, with this difference: we can leave this interior dwelling through sin, since we cannot be absolutely sinless here below, as the saints are in Heaven.

IV

To assist at Holy Mass well
we must be united to Jesus Christ

I AM IN DOUBT, my Sisters: Do we Religious, having more acquaintance with the Mysteries of God than ordinary people, fulfill our obligation to assist at holy Mass when our minds are not intent on the sacrifice? Jesus, as the Head of Christians, is there offered for all, and I am convinced we are obliged to assist there as members united to their Head. Consequently, we should have not only the intention of hearing Holy Mass, but an explicit intention of doing what Jesus does, who sacrifices us with Himself. We should present ourselves at the altar with Jesus Christ and enter into His dispositions through Him. I mean to say, insinuate ourselves, sweetly and simply, into the motives of His sacrifice, into His intentions, into His designs, and into the effects this sacrifice should produce. When we lack these intentions, we do not participate well in Mass and the sacrifice does not have the fullness on our part which we should bring to it through the dispositions and unity just described, because if one member is separated from the Head, the body is not whole. Without a doubt, Jesus is perfect in His natural and personal Body; but in His mystical Body there are often members cut off and it is an infinite sorrow to Jesus that anyone should be so separated from Him.

Hear the complaints and lamentations He made one day to one of His spouses, who desired to console His most lovable Heart's inner sorrows during His agony on the Cross. "My daughter," He said, "you should know that the cruelest of My

27

interior sufferings was the separation of My mystical members (the Christian people) from My Heart. This suffering was so painful to Me that without a miracle of My omnipotence, I could not have borne it without dying. I saw souls who tore themselves away from Me and those who will tear themselves away until the end of the world and My Heart, broken with an infinite love for each soul, had to suffer death from the violent and terrible sorrow it experienced from this tearing away." Then He added, "Picture, my daughter, the sight of an executed criminal pulled by four horses. He is quartered, and the members torn apart; this is but the faintest shadow of My pain, since the torments which he suffers in being quartered are infinitely far from my martyrdom and the extreme anguish I endured in that separation. Nothing is capable of expressing it because the love and tenderness I have for My Elect is infinite."

Judge, my Sisters, from the little I just said, the kind of union we have with Jesus Christ, and how painful our separation is to Him. Next, consider whether it is true that being part of His body, we should be sacrificed with Him and that those who are not, are, in fact, separated members and consequently are dead, since they are not animated by the life of the Head. To fulfill our obligation and not renew the cruel sorrow of Jesus Christ, we should abide in Him; through union, intention, and attention, we should do with Him what He does, especially in the Holy Mass, which is the mystery of our reconciliation and sanctification. Oh! How many souls in the infernal depths would not have fallen into evil if they had even once assisted at Mass as they should? They would have received efficacious graces for their conversion and return to God, and the power to remove themselves from vice.

But what an appalling disaster! We attend Mass with distracted minds, without reverence, and without thinking about the immense graces God is communicating to us there.

Is it such a little thing, then, the blood of a God poured out? God Himself is sacrificed there for us to merit heaven, to obtain pardon for our sins, and to appease the divine justice which would strike us at every moment if this Lamb slain from the foundation of the world did not offer Himself to carry the weight of His just wrath against sinners, and if He did not take on Himself the chastisement we merit for our infidelities. Let us frequently offer Jesus under the appearance of the Host, in Himself glorious, thus thanking Him for His love for us, and let us begin to make a pure use of it.

Everything in the most holy Sacrifice of the Mass is infinite. The victim offered is the Son of God, a Person of infinite merit. This divine Son is sacrificed for the glory of God His Father, infinite in all His perfections, God offered to God. This infinite Son is the first and principal Priest and Sacrificer who offers Himself to His Father in His own person, and by the hands of the priest. It is He who by the mouth of His minister pronounces the sacramental words which accomplish this Mystery: "This is My Body." That is why in Psalm 109 He is called "eternal priest" by His Father. That infinite Son sacrifices Himself in a way which is entirely perfect and beyond human understanding. This is why a single Mass, even one celebrated by a wicked priest, gives more glory to God than all the praises of men and angels.

Jesus Christ prepared for thirty-three years to celebrate a single time the divine Eucharistic Sacrifice.

During the celebration of Holy Mass, the Altar is surrounded by angels and seraphim, who descend in order to adore and admire the profound annihilation to which love has reduced their King and Sovereign. And although this divine sacrifice is not offered for them, they adore Jesus Christ there with inconceivable reverence, and admire the high dignity of priests; they have a holy envy of them and are enraptured by the excessive love for men which this gracious and sovereign Lord demonstrates in this Mystery.

Let us now discuss the way to assist at Mass well, although it is difficult to set up systems on this matter, inasmuch as there are as many different ways as there are different souls; each one acts according to its degree of elevation and union with Jesus Christ.

Those who have just begun the work of the interior life need instruction and set prayers, to habituate them to filling themselves with the sacred mystery of which the holy Mass is the living re-presentation. Others, more enlightened, should learn how to unite themselves to Jesus sacrificed in the divine Host and how to follow all the parts of His sacrifice. Finally, the most elevated souls enter in union and are with Jesus the Host by state. These last have no need of systems, since they should remain simply in Jesus, whom they see in themselves. All they have to do is live in continual death and allow themselves to be animated by His life, not through the flow of grace, as with other states, but from Him; that is to say, with the same life He lives in Himself.[13] The soul enters into this state by a singular mercy; she sees nothing other than Him and does nothing outside of Him, but acts in a completely divine manner. This is only understood by souls who are established in this state and who experience this unity. Since one cannot enter into this state through study, there is no need of rules for those who are in it. Each soul should walk her path with a profound humility, remembering the words of the Savior who urges us to choose the last place when we are invited to the wedding feast.[14]

---

[13] Mother Mectilde seems to be distinguishing here between actual grace and sanctifying grace (God's own life shared with the soul, producing an abiding state of union), though she does not use that language.

[14] Luke 14:10.

My Sisters, I find that the Holy Sacrifice of the Mass is a most magnificent feast, for there the flesh of God is eaten and we drink His Blood, so that the souls of the guests are completely filled with Jesus Christ; namely, we are filled with His divinity and with His humanity, with His holy soul and all His infinite perfections, and by concomitance, with the Father and the Holy Spirit. This is what is given to us in this precious mystery which, for being too common, is neglected, and for being so excellent, is understood by only a few.

Nevertheless we assist at Mass every day, but truthfully, with too little fruit. This grieves and astonishes me. What! Is it possible that we assist at the death of God, at the shedding of His Blood, at the reconciliation He makes for us with His Father, and we remain so cold, so distracted, and so far from Jesus? We must say the same thing about Holy Communion, because the fault we commit in the one, we commit again in the other.

We should keep watch over three externals when attending holy Mass: first, modesty of the body; second, respectful posture, as much as weakness permits; and third, silence, never speaking to anyone during so fearful a mystery. With regard to internal dispositions, we should have a profound humility, a lively faith, and recollection in all the soul's powers. Amazement should hold the mind and love should seize the will. But we should never hear Mass without first having made an act of contrition, detesting sin in ourselves and in our neighbor, since it is the cause of the death of God which you go to see on the mystical Calvary, where He went to be immolated. Let us enter into this sacred mystery in the name of God.

Here is the way all Christians should participate in the Holy Mass; it is the easiest and unites us most to Jesus.

I assume that we have taken a little time to prepare ourselves in the aforementioned dispositions; before the celebration of the mystery, the space of a *Miserere* is sufficient if used well.

31

Regard the priest as Jesus Christ or see Jesus Christ in the priest. He ascends to the altar and then he descends. This procession you may understand as His path from the Cenacle to the Garden of Olives. The priest genuflects, to remind us how He knelt before the majesty of His Father, whom He adores and prays to at the altar. We should enter with Him into the same attitude of reverence which humbles Jesus before the infinite greatness of God. We should adore it with Him, and like Him, with the same intention and with love for all that He does, all that He suffers, and what He says.

This first step is capable of keeping souls occupied, not only during holy Mass, but throughout all of life, since it contains infinite depths. However, we must acknowledge our terrible ignorance about these divine mysteries; it is often the reason for our dryness, our poverty, our distracted minds and the little fruit which we obtain.

The holy Mass is the living re-presentation of the sacrifice of the Cross. And we have an absolute obligation to apply it to ourselves, following the command which Our Lord gives us by the mouth of the priest, who says, *quotiescumque feceritis, in meam memoriam facietis.*[15] We must therefore renew this sorrowful Mystery; it is His intention, and the reason He instituted the Sacrifice of the Altar. He wants to renew it every day before His Father, in order to restore the glory which our sins have stolen from Him and make satisfaction to His offended justice. He also renews it within our hearts in order to light a new flame of His love in them; since this infinite love which He has for us keeps Him in subjection and makes Him obey so punctually the voice of the priest when he says, "*Hoc est corpus meum.*"[16]

---

[15] "As often as you do these things, ye shall do them in remembrance of Me." Luke 22:19; 1 Corinthians 11:24.

[16] "This is My Body." Luke 22:19, Matt. 26:26–28, Mark 14:22–24.

It seems to me that although it is permissible to have other good thoughts during the holy Mass, they are not entirely conformed to the intentions of Jesus if they do not have likeness and unity with His sacrifice. In fact, how would it be to see Him on the altar, immolated as truly as on Calvary, saying to us by the voice of His outpoured Blood, "I die and I sacrifice Myself anew at every hour and every moment for you": can you think of something other than this infinite love which took away His life? However, we can meditate upon the different parts of the sacrifice of Calvary and of the altar; each one may follow the attractions of grace, without leaving the mystery. It can be that the meekness of Jesus occupies the soul, or we may consider His silence in the midst of His enemies and accusers; how He makes no response when they insult and injure Him, *Jesus autem tacebat.*[17] We can adore and remain in Him in these various scenes, which are very fruitful. Some touch upon His profound annihilation, others on His patience before the insults He received from the wicked, or His humility when He said of Himself, *Ego sum vermis.*[18] They feel pierced by His gentleness, by His infinite charity, by the pardon which He begs for His executioners, and so on. Some souls are drawn to honor the wounds of His sacred Heart and the agonies of His holy soul; His dereliction on the Cross, the rigor of the holiness of the Father on this God-Man become victim. Others envisage and adore Him as the Lamb of God who takes away the sins of the world or as the Mediator who reconciles us with His Father, as a Host of propitiation, and as a divine Holocaust, which is consumed in the odor of sweetness before the supreme majesty of God. One can adore Him as a divine Lover, whom love carried even to infinite excess,

[17] "But Jesus was silent." Matthew 26:63.
[18] "I am a worm and no man." Psalm 21:7.

as a God in some way lost among sinners and prostitutes, abandoned to every sort of shame, contempt, and sorrow, to save men; an unknown without consolation from any creature, dying between two thieves. We can adore His bloody wounds, and faint with love at the opening of his adorable Heart, or remain at His feet with the loving Magdalene, pierced, like her, with an immense sorrow, collecting the tears and the blood coming from this divine Pelican to feed His little ones, or hearing the seven words He spoke from the Cross, which contain the summary of all evangelic perfection. One can also descend into Limbo with the soul of Jesus, or expire with Him, saying, "*In manus tuas, Domine, commendo spiritum meum,*"[19] receiving Him into one's heart as into the sepulcher, to remain hidden there with Him in a spirit of death.

We would never finish, if we wished to speak of all that is contained in the august sacrifice of the Altar; it is a subject which contains infinite riches, which we must leave to the piety of souls whom the Holy Spirit wishes to instruct. I say only that we must be united with the Son of God, and in no way separated from Him, and that the souls who are not in this state of union should renew themselves in it at the beginning of the Mass, trying to enter into it as they can, in order to render the sacrifice fully accomplished, as we have shown elsewhere.

After an act of simple faith and profound humility, looking to Jesus, believe that you are truly present at this great and awesome sacrifice which astonishes the angels and engulfs the most exalted of the seraphim in nothingness. All of heaven trembles and shudders in horror, seeing God reduced to the image of a criminal, and charged with the abominable sins of

---

[19] "Into your hands, O Lord, I commend my spirit." Psalm 30:6; Luke 23:46.

the whole world. Here Jesus is in the greatest humiliation possible. It is in this state of shame that He is annihilated before the divine holiness and that He makes a fitting atonement[20] and an act of hatred for sin so perfect that He merits pardon for the sins of men. Here Jesus appears as a criminal although He is sinless. Here He is treated with all the rigor of divine justice and holiness; He is made our victim and the ransom for sinners. Here He receives the sentence of death and enters into agonies, seeing the inconceivable sufferings of His body and soul. It is here that He bestows Himself on souls, each one in particular; here He accepts death in order to give us life. Here He restores the rights which sin had stolen from us; here He merits for us the grace to enter into commerce with His Father; He teaches us to detest sin and impresses us with its horror. It is here that the Father did not pardon His own Son and that God is annihilated before the supreme majesty of the infinite God. Here all creatures rise against Jesus, made sin, as St. Paul says,[21] in order to avenge the injury which the sinner did to God by his sin. Here Jesus the God-Man is abandoned to the power of darkness and reduced to the last extremity, saying "*Tristis est anima mea usque ad mortem.*"[22] Here He waters the ground with His Blood, and He meets such suffering that He is reduced to the agonies of death. Here all sins

---

[20] *Amende honorable.* In the past in France, this was a mode of punishment which required the offender to be led barefoot by the public executioner into a church or other public place, with a torch in hand and a rope around his neck, to beg pardon of his God, his king, and his country on his knees. It came to have the meaning of reparation and satisfactory apology. For Mother Mectilde's adaptation of this punishment within her monastic foundations, see page 87, note 47.

[21] 2 Corinthians 5:21.

[22] "My soul is sorrowful even unto death." Matthew 26:38, Mark 14:34.

come in a throng upon this divine Savior in order to cover Him with their infamous darkness; in this state He comes before divine justice, which will take from Him all the satisfaction which is due to it, in all strictness, and in a complete slaking, if one may use such a term. The holy soul of Jesus suffers not only this mortal repugnance at the approach of sin, but further a great and extreme fear, terror, and dismay, which sin encounters from God, in the fury of His wrath. And this fury and terror are as great as the light of the Son of God is full and penetrating, to make known what sin is before God and what God is contrary to sin; this is what a righteous God inflicted on sin in order to be avenged.

All these things, and many others, my Sisters, which I leave to your thoughts, show you the infinite sufferings of Jesus, the only Son of God, about which He had good reason to say by a prophet: *Circumdederunt me dolores mortis*;[23] for these sufferings are as vast as the sea, where His Heart drowns and sinks. The sorrows of death surrounded Me, I am submerged in the flood of all the sins of the whole world; the pains of hell besiege Me. He would have died in fact, if the omnipotent hand of God had not sustained His life in order to keep Him for the shameful death of the Cross.

We should honor and meditate on all the phases of the Passion when assisting at Mass. Though I have spoken in detail only of the events of the Garden of Olives, I do not mean that souls should stop there. Rather, this shows the holy way to nourish the mind with each aspect of the Passion of Our Lord, of which the Holy Sacrifice of the Mass is the memorial. There are infinite things to be found in this which require our adoration and our imitation, humbling us with Jesus Christ and consuming us in His sacrifice.

[23] Psalm 114:3.

V

On Confession

THE BEST DISPOSITION we can bring to the Sacrament of Penance is a profound humility, through which the soul sincerely realizes that she is sinful and thus unworthy to appear before the majesty of a holy God whose eyes are infinitely pure.

Secondly, we should consider Our Lord Jesus Christ in the Garden of Olives, bent under the weight of the world's sins, sweating blood and water, making acts of the most acute sorrow imaginable and alone capable of satisfying divine justice. We should not pass lightly over this state of the Savior. He is there in the position of a criminal, despite being innocence itself, and as the Prince of the Apostles said, "He committed no sin, no guile was found on His lips."[24] But He bore our sins in His own body, He was covered with the shame which is their due, and entered into the abyss of nothingness. Therefore, when we go to confess, we should look upon ourselves as sinners, my Sisters. In reality we are, by the commission of a great number of sins, whereas Our Master had only the appearance of a sinner and He was only our ransom; nevertheless He was rejected by His Father and underwent the condemnation of sinners. The Son was handed over to torment and death in order to deliver the slaves. God's justice in anger discharges upon this Lamb all the darts of its fury, and makes Him pay the debts which He had in no way con-

[24] 1 Peter 2:22.

tracted, according to the expression of the Psalmist in Psalm 68.[25]

It would be difficult to express the suffering of the Son of God in this condition. He suffered in reality all the pains which sinners ought to experience were they enlightened enough to understand the evil of sin. The Eternal Father treated Him as a blasphemer, a murderer, a false witness, a perjurer, and so on, and He appeared in His eyes covered with the filth of all the abominations of men. Oh, God! What an object! The pain caused Him by the rebukes of His Father was so great that, notwithstanding His zeal for the Father's glory and for the salvation of souls, He cried, "My Father, if it is possible, let this Chalice pass without My tasting its bitterness; nevertheless Thy will be done."[26] His lower part desired that God would be satisfied with His extreme agony. But the sentence of death was pronounced, He must die. St. Paul says something which captures all that one can think about this subject: "*exinanavit semetipsum*,"[27] He annihilated Himself. Yes, through His love, He made Himself a disgrace and the outcast of God and of all creatures; since each one according to its capacity conspired in His death, in order to avenge the dishonor which sin had done to God. A God covered with the form of a sinner, charged with all the sins of the world. Oh! What an unfathomable mystery! Who can understand it? My Sisters, it is for us that Jesus Christ bore that title; it is for us that He was rejected and condemned. This is what we ought

[25] "I pay that which I did not take away." Psalm 68:5. In the Latin Vulgate: *quae non rapui, tunc exsolvebam.*

[26] Matthew 26:39.

[27] "He emptied Himself." Philippians 2:7. This is the precise meaning of *anéanti* when applied to Christ—the kenotic self-emptying humility of His incarnation, crucifixion, and presence under the Eucharistic species.

to be, and yet we do not think about it. Let us wake from the sleep of ignorance and idleness, and enter into the practice of such a holy hatred of sin, which Jesus exercised for us. Yes, in truth, it is for us that He is contrite and humiliated and that He bears the rebukes of God which we have merited. He did the penance that we were not capable of doing. He is our ransom and cried out for us; He paid for our acquittal. We should at least enter into His holy dispositions and not render useless the grace He merited for us.

When we present ourselves at the tribunal of penance, we must be in some disposition which has a resemblance to that of Jesus. We should enter into the most holy and most perfect horror of sin which He had, and into the humiliation to which He found Himself reduced before the greatness of His Father, a sorrow and abasement so profound that He remained prostrate and as if annihilated. This is how we should be at the feet of the priest who represents Our Lord for us. We should bring a heart broken with regret for our sins, and a spirit humbled even to the center of the abyss; we should apply to ourselves what Jesus Christ Our Lord did and suffered in the Garden of Olives, abandoning ourselves to His grace and His love in order to receive some of its effects, offering to the Eternal Father the sufferings of His Son in satisfaction for those we lack.

However, my Sisters, beware of scruples and anxiety about your previous confessions, for God is as good as He is just. Do not be troubled about your past life; it is necessary to humble ourselves but not to torture ourselves. Let your bitterness be peaceful: always hating your disorders, but not wasting time in dwelling on them. We must indeed have regret for our infidelities and the poor use we have made of the Blood of Jesus Christ, but without any distrust of His mercy.

All the Fathers are in agreement that the prodigal son of the

Gospel is the figure of the penitent sinner, who, after removing himself from God by his sins, came back with sorrow in his heart, tears in his eyes, and these words in his mouth: "My Father, I have sinned against heaven and against you. I am not worthy to be called your son, treat me only as a poor servant." Oh how powerful humility is for drawing down graces from heaven! Does it not seem to enchant the Lord and tie the hands of His justice? He cannot prevent Himself from coming to meet this prodigal soul and treating him as did the father in the parable just mentioned. He receives him with mercy, he embraces him, he gives him the best robe, he puts a ring on his hand and sandals on his feet, and he has the fatted calf killed to feast with his friends, as a sign of rejoicing over the return of his prodigal child. And all the angels take part in this feast, for the conversion of one sinner is a reason for their charity and joy. Let us be converted then, to our divine Father. Let us ask Him to grant that we may be the slaves of His servants, being unworthy of the title of children, taking humiliation for our portion and never leaving it; whatever eminence and advantages we may have, let us dwell in nothingness.

I knew a soul of grace whom Our Lord commanded to enter this [nothingness]. From that time, she has never left it. She says that the nothingness of being and the nothingness of sin are her noble origins and that the wrath of God and eternal damnation were her birthright. What can we think about her origin, her dignity, her excellence? In reality, on what can we establish our eminence? We would be ridiculous and unreasonable if we were not continually confounded, since we have nothing in ourselves besides causes for horror and annihilation. I like humble souls very much, provided they beware of anxiety and eagerness; instead they should remain only in the spirit of compunction.

We should go to confession with simplicity and trust,

accusing ourselves of our faults in few words; with the intention of doing homage to the justice and holiness of God and by no means for personal interest, or for the unburdening of our consciences of the weight and pain caused by sin. It is certain that our ignorance robs us of seeing the majority of our infidelities. This is why they should be detested even without our being aware of them, as the products of the wicked ground of impurity and darkness which we inherited from Adam. We should receive the penance imposed on us with a profound reverence and submission, and work towards our amendment with courage, since our conversion should be the fruit of the Sacrament of Penance.

VI

The dispositions we should have when approaching Holy Communion

WE SHOULD GO to Holy Communion, my Sisters, (1) so that Our Lord may be in us all that He ought to be and so that we may cease to be all that we are, with the intention of being blessedly lost in Him and separated from ourselves.

(2) Also, so that in coming to us, He may destroy all that is contrary to God, such as the generation of Adam and its rebellion, the reign of sin, the empire of the evil spirit and our domination which usurps us by self-love, [instead] producing in our souls perfect justice, crucifying the old man, and establishing God's reign. Thus, our imperfections should make us desire Holy Communion out of zeal to destroy them.

(3) The gifts and graces which it pleases God to give us should be quickened by Holy Communion so that it may please Our Lord to come and take possession of His favors and mercies and so that by our malignity we do not usurp this realm and appropriate it for our own use.

We should go to the holy Table out of obedience to the desire of Jesus Christ Our Lord to receive us into Himself, into His life and being, destroying our present life and being, so that He may make us what He is, namely: life, love, truth, virtue for God. Also we should go out of submission to His will for us to be members animated with His life, for the glory of His Father, and which can be used in the works pertaining to it.

We owe obedience to the desires of this divine Savior, who

wants to receive us and take possession of our souls. For Holy Communion does not only give Jesus to us, it also gives us to Him, according to this prophetic utterance pronounced by His lips, "The one who eats My flesh and drinks My Blood abides in Me and I in him."[28] Now, the desire of Jesus to receive us is as great as His charity, which is exceedingly great, and as great as His merits which give Him rights and kingship over us. It is a great infidelity to deprive Him of the fulfillment of His desires, unless we have some involuntary impediment which we cannot overcome.

It is an excellent preparation for Holy Communion to be nothing, to desire nothing, to be able to do nothing, bringing to it only a total abandonment of self; leaving oneself to the power of Jesus in the Most Holy Sacrament, in order to be reclothed with His mercy and with Himself, in the way He intends, and not according to our own ideas and the desires of our senses. We must live as Jesus lived for His Father; it is His intention that we live from Him and for Him.

Let us go to God, my Sisters, with trust and love and not hold back from motives of fear. Alas! What presumption to think that we could prepare ourselves for Communion in a manner worthy of this great Sacrament! God alone can prepare us for it by His grace and mercy. We have nothing, then, my Sisters, unless the Lord gives it to us. Present yourselves before His divine presence in order to receive what it pleases Him to give you; ask Jesus to receive Himself in the depths of your heart, and to glorify Himself there in the way that will be most pleasing, since you are incapable of doing so. Ask Him that His love may make up for you and receive Communion in this humble, simple, and loving disposition.

---

[28] John 6:57.

The dispositions we should have

After Holy Communion, remain in silence and faith, in reverence and love, above your feelings. Do not be surprised that you feel absolutely nothing, that you have nothing to say, or have no fine thoughts. You do not go to Communion in order to find life in yourselves but to find death. Leave yourselves in death then, so that God can give you life from Himself. Remain in a peaceful acquiescence toward all He does in you and all that He wants from you and continuing in this holy abandonment and in real sacrifice, you will be doing what God wants and you will not put up any obstacle to His work. Do not listen to the complaints of your senses, or to the reasoning of your mind; this must all die, they are all impure and sinful. Pay them no attention and remain sacrificed to the good pleasure and love of Jesus Christ.

It is not enough to have this disposition only during Holy Communion; we should have it afterwards and we should continue it in all the actions of life. Thus we will be always in a state of abandonment so that the grace which accompanies it [viz., Communion] may be poured out unceasingly in all our conduct. Let us remain in the condition of victim which Jesus has in the Most Holy Sacrament, desiring to be conformed to Him as much as possible for a creature.

Undoubtedly, we will never be worthy of Communion, having no such disposition within ourselves. But Jesus Christ, by His [part in] Communion, has sanctified ours and merited for us the grace to participate in His heavenly banquet. Let us not render this grace fruitless, let us go to Him in spite of our poverty (assuming that there is no other reason which obliges us to do so than this lack), thinking less about our darkness than the desire we should have to give ourselves to Jesus Christ. Let us cease the use we have made of ourselves and the usurpation of His rights over us. Let us deliver ourselves entirely to His holy disposition, satisfied that God in Himself is enough and that He is contented with us as He pleases, without our feelings taking part. Let us be faithful and this divine sun will give the light and warmth with which He is accompanied in the august Sacrament when it pleases Him. We should never grow weary of waiting for it; humility, meekness, and patience will attract it at last to the depth of our hearts. I pray that He live in them and establish His Kingdom there forever.

VII

On Holy Communion in general

MY SISTERS, it would be desirable if someone were able to speak about the adorable Sacrifice Our Lord Jesus Christ offers in the soul during the time of Holy Communion, which happens in the most intimate depth of the soul, and about the dispositions the soul should have so that she creates no obstacle to this precious mystery which operates in such a divine manner. However, I have neither the grace nor the light to speak about it. One must be conducted into the *sancta sanctorum* of the soul where this God of infinite majesty resides and produces miraculous effects from those ineffable unions. All that I can say is that I believe there are mysteries which happen in Holy Communion, which the souls who communicate do not understand at all.

If we must speak about the necessary preparations, which I acknowledge must be done, we should encourage souls who are beginning the interior life to be properly disposed. However, if we may reason about what we can do, what are our dispositions, our desires, our ardors, and all the rest? Although they appear to be good, alas, we consider these things quite unworthy of the purity and holiness of Jesus Christ; all that we can produce is tainted and comes from a depth which is corrupt and damaged. While it seems to be very pure and most excellent, what can we say, what can we bring forth, in order to appear before His infinite greatness?

Without condemning the opinions of others, I believe that the best we can do is to be silent, to abase ourselves, to sink

47

into the ground of our nothingness, to acknowledge it by faith even if we do not feel it, and remain infinitely (if that were possible) retired before that supreme Majesty. My view is that the soul should remain withdrawn, so to speak, in her unworthiness, as if she did not dare to be seen because of what she is through sin. She will remain thus engulfed in her nothingness, while Jesus Christ enters the soul, and into which He descends as a King into his domain, to whom everything belongs and in whose presence each person must draw back to make room for Him. What is meant by this withdrawal into ourselves? It is that the spirit is humbled, cast down, remaining in the confession of its nothingness, of its infinite unworthiness; and the mind thus abashed, the senses are consequently barred, they do not dare to approach that august Majesty. You will bear with this little observation of mine, that those of us who are anxious during our Communions are that way because the mind and the senses are not content, since their tastes are not satisfied; they are not brought to the feast, they are not invited to the banquet hall; ordinarily the mind perceives nothing of it and so the senses remain in dryness. This is marvelous, although painful to bear. The soul, which lives only a sensitive and animal life, knows nothing about this divine life which Jesus Christ has just given by means of the Holy Eucharist. And since this divine bread is not perceptible to the senses, the soul is convinced it should have some heavenly taste, and that she should experience it, and to be inebriated with the delights it contains, which many saintly souls have enjoyed in Holy Communion.

We must make a distinction in order to avoid confusion about what we should say. It is true, there are some souls who receive Communion with sweetness and pleasure although they have still done or suffered almost nothing for Jesus Christ. Of these there are two classes: in the first, innocence preserved makes them enjoy some passing delights, but this has almost no other effect than keeping the soul from falling into some great sin. Second, some souls can only serve God because of these favors, without which they would not cleave to His love; they are like sinners, like those who are only interested in sensual pleasures, and so on. These work for pay, they are mercenary. However, there is a third class and these are souls purified in the furnace of very harsh treatment from God, by immense suffering, by trials, by temptations and the like. After this purification is fully accomplished, Jesus Christ reproduces Himself in the soul's depths and bestows indescribable joys on their senses. But alas! Before this how many awful deaths! How many long agonies and cruel sufferings! Those whom God has resurrected from the dead can indeed live the life of Jesus Christ. But do you think these are very common? I believe them to be as rare as a phoenix among birds. But why so rare? Because one cannot find anybody who wants to endure the rigor of the consuming fire which must purify them through extreme poverty, through rejections, and so on.

Let us leave those perfect souls to speak of a more ordinary state, where the majority of souls stop. They complain and fret that they do nothing in Holy Communion and that they are not benefitting at all from such a grace. If you were to ask them the cause, they do not know. "I go to confession," they say, "I do what I can and nevertheless I am very miserable." I would like to make a further distinction in the different degrees of these souls troubled about Holy Communion. To tell the truth, there are as many states of soul as there are persons who go to Communion. Some are dry because of daily infidelities which they make no effort to correct; others are poor due to ignorance and will not take trouble to read in order to fill their minds with good thoughts and keep them occupied. For, we must note something very important: first, in order to receive Holy Communion well, the soul must do all she can on her part to keep herself not only from mortal sin but also from deliberate venial sin, and do as much as possible to root out her bad habits such as pride, vanity, and the like. Second, she must try to remain recollected during the day, while faithful to her regular duties. Third, she should never miss an occasion given by Providence for the solid practice of the virtues. These three points must be established in a soul; I do not say that she must be perfect, but I am assuming she does what she can.

I come now to Holy Communion where these souls complain about their dryness, poverty, and powerlessness. Not knowing what to do with their minds, their memory, will, and senses, which are all oppressed, they cry out sorrowfully. Due to their difficulties they suffer temptations which are already in the soul through other means to disturb it and make it anxious; these bring a million terrible thoughts of every kind, often of despair and condemnation. What advice will we give souls thus afflicted? Oh! If only it were easy to satisfy them; if only they would have a little docility of mind to believe what we tell them in their troubles and if only they wanted do what they are taught. I have no doubt, though it would not be the first or second day, that they would find marvelous graces hidden in the depth of their poverty and anguish. Oh! If only they would resolve to ignore themselves a little in this condition, if they would stand aloof from themselves a little, not by force, but by patience; if they would attempt to let all of these extravagant thoughts, impressions, temptations, and so on pass by.

If someone says to me, "I cannot be rid of it," I would answer that I do not mean that, but only that they bear with patience the thoughts which come and go, whether of insolence, blasphemy, impiety, etc. You must let all this pass without examining it. "But," you will say, "I cannot. I am, so to speak, forced to think of these things without being able to separate myself from them." I want to believe that you are not able to defend yourself from hearing their noise, seeing their malice, and feeling their tyranny. Well then, it is a cause for patience. This is not something you think about willingly. "It seems," you will reply, "that my will is completely bound, that it is pleased by it, that it wants to sin and that I am an abomination, etc." I grant that your will appears to be engaged in it; but know that you have two wills, the higher, and the lower which we call appetite, and one is only easily distinguished from the other by souls who master themselves peacefully. These souls must have patience and simply believe what they are told. Oh! if they knew the great harm they do by not submitting their mind and judgment to this guidance, they would die of sorrow rather than ever fail to do so. You must be abandoned simply and when the storm is so violent that all is overturned and lost, you must find your repose in your own suffering.[29]

But let us move forward, and say what Our Lord does in a poor and afflicted soul, and which has no means of entry into the royal chamber, or of taking part in the feast. Oh! Sisters, this is the mystery of mysteries; for us, Jesus Christ enters the soul in Holy Communion, without any need for the soul to

---

[29] *Manuscript variant*: …in your own ruin. "What! In hell? Since I would be damned." Yes, in hell; since we must believe that God executes justice, and you are bound to His interests, letting your own die. These would not allow an eternal separation from God, not based on the pure love which you have for Him, but from the secret instinct of your self-love. Be abandoned, then, to the good pleasure of God, be it justice or mercy; for insofar as the soul is not in this holy abandonment, she makes no progress and does not fulfill the plan of Jesus Christ for her interior purgation. But let us…

prepare the chamber or open the *sancta sanctorum* to which He withdraws. I know that entering into our breast, He passes into that holy sanctuary in the intimate part of ourselves, where He renews His adorable mysteries, and principally that of His sacrifice, in a way very beneficial to the soul. For Jesus, being substantially united to us by the divine Eucharist, we become (in the opinion of the Fathers) one and the same with Him, because we are bone of His bones, flesh of His Flesh[30] and so united to Him that this union fills the whole Church with astonishment, she cannot understand it or admire it enough. This is *de fide* and we must believe it.

Now, I ask you, when you receive Communion, is it you who cause this union or transformation? Certainly not, it is Jesus by virtue of His divine Sacrament. It is enough on your part that you are in a state of grace and the rest is done by the infinite love of Jesus Christ. This being true and *de fide*, why is it that we teach nothing to souls about the way to act and what they should do during this divine exchange? I say that they need do almost nothing: only two things. First, they should adhere to Jesus in the depth of their will; second, they should not interfere by wanting to enter and perceive what is happening in themselves, in order to feel it; they only need to remain recollected as much as they can, and simply consent to what is happening in the soul through the divine and personal power of Jesus Christ. If the soul cannot remain peaceful or has neither reverence nor attention, then she should say, many times, along with the Church, with all her heart, *Amen*. This word is powerful and mysterious. It is a vow and a consent which the soul gives to all that God does in His Church and all that the Church does towards God. It is fitting to say it often with this intention, since the Church also causes it to be

[30] Cf. Genesis 2:23.

repeated many times. This word has its origin in the Church Triumphant. St. John indicates this to us when describing the four animals and the twenty-four elders, who are prostrated before the throne of the Lamb, responding *Amen* to all the praises, adoration, worship, and blessings given to the Living God and to the One who alone has the power to open the book sealed with seven seals, who is none other than Jesus Christ, the divine Lamb slain from the foundation of the world. It is not said that the twenty-four Princes of the Apocalypse utter anything other than this precious word, which also contains an agreement and pure consent to all the operations of Jesus Christ and to the effects which happen in the soul, though unknown to her.

What does the soul become by Communion, then? Jesus Christ. But although Jesus Christ, I sense nothing, see nothing, experience nothing. No, because this transformation is accomplished in the substance of our soul, and though your body is also transformed, you can neither see nor experience this transformation or this divine operation unless God reveals it to you, as I know He has done to some. But although you see and feel nothing, it is true and infallible. We must believe it, and it is the happiness of the soul to remain in faith, and to live in ignorance, in order to have a more profound submission to such incomprehensible Mysteries.

Jesus Christ, being thus in the soul, where does He withdraw? As I said, to the *sancta sanctorum* of the soul, which is the intimate depths and which serves as a sanctuary for this High Priest and as a temple where He celebrates His divine and redoubtable sacrifice of all Himself to His Father. This sacrifice He wants to renew in the depth of each soul as in a holy temple, which He consecrated on the day of its Baptism. O inconceivable marvel! Jesus Christ descends into our hearts to be immolated and to celebrate there His solemn Mass, although in profound silence. Everything is quiet in that temple, the angels and saints admire and adore the abasements of Jesus Christ. And the Eternal Father is well pleased.

But how does this sacrifice benefit the soul? By the sacrifice itself; since, being substantially united, the soul cannot be separated from Jesus Christ, and consequently, the soul is immolated with Him and by Him in this temple. The soul forms part of His sacrifice which she could never do except by Holy Communion. My Sisters, this is the miraculous and wonderful invention of Jesus Christ, to give the soul the means to be offered through Him to the Eternal Father, in a manner worthy of His greatness. In this divine Mystery the soul is in no way separated from Jesus Christ. And since the Eternal Father receives Him with an infinite satisfaction, we can say that He also receives the soul united to Jesus Christ, since there is no separation between Jesus Christ and the soul through the blessed Sacrament.

Given this truth, why fret so much that we do nothing in Holy Communion? In truth, all that you can do there, does it come anywhere near what Jesus does for you? Therefore, you have only to unite yourself to Him, consenting to all He does, and to adore Him in silence, or with a few words full of reverence, and submit. Oh! If the soul could know the good it does by withdrawing, could we not say: Holy Communion is always very agreeable to her, because then the soul would be convinced that it is a mystery which works in her, almost without her, since everything is done by Jesus Christ. If one would give oneself to this holy practice, the soul would receive wonderful effects from this sacrifice, she will be changed without thinking about it. She will experience an indescribable divine power which will detach her from self, from creatures, from imperfections, and everything else. This is incomprehensible and I cannot explain it sufficiently myself.

It would be relevant to describe here the structure of the mysterious temple where Jesus and the soul form a single sacrifice and a single oblation, but I would not finish. It is enough to show that a soul which, by the grace of God, is free of mortal sin, participates in Jesus Christ in this way. As for those whose lives are purer, they receive, without doubt, more sensible and wonderful effects.

We must note two or three things about all we have said, in order to prevent the difficulty this could cause in some souls who do not practice mortification. They will say that if Jesus alone causes this divine transformation, then they do not need to keep their minds recollected, or take any trouble to prepare for Holy Communion, according to what they can and should do on their part. We must keep in mind that this divine operation requires a faithful correspondence, and a continual vigilance, in order to live in the purity and holiness of such a grace. Consequently, it requires the faithful practice of mortification and destruction of oneself; otherwise, such a prodigious favor will accomplish nothing in us of the sanctification which is proper to it and which Jesus intends as the effect of this adorable Sacrament. Therefore, it is not enough to be united to Jesus Christ only in Communion, we must bear the fruits of this union in the practice of the virtues of patience, obedience, meekness, humility, charity, and so forth.

It is also relevant to know that silence must be observed at the time of Holy Communion, as I have said, and afterwards as well; this is not an indolent silence, since it contains attention and profound reverence for the greatness of God; and though this reverence does not make an impression on the senses, it will not fail to have its effect. Second, it is an adoring silence, for if you keep watch on the interior movements in this recollection, the entire ground of the soul is turned toward God, giving itself to Him, adhering to Him, loving

Him, and so forth. But when the poor soul is troubled with pains and temptations, she is not able to discern it [viz., this adherence], and believes that she does nothing but waste time, or dishonor that infinite Majesty. The fruitful souls who are filled with good sentiments, very good; they pour these out before the Lord's throne, as is right. But for those who are sterile, poor, blind, and powerless, if they simply follow the advice given above, the practice will become very fruitful to them. What I have said concerns only the poor, timid souls who are pained or scrupulous, believing they waste time, and so on. It can happen sometimes that they will be restricted, even by a movement of grace, without discerning it; but they should leave themselves to the working of Jesus, sacrificing their souls with Him, being content to adhere simply to all that He does in them. Little by little the soul which practices this without being attached to her own senses will find a change in her interior: more calm and more clarity, although this exercise seems to obscure the understanding, keeping it captive and subject, not allowing the soul to trouble about seeing and knowing. It is much better for the soul to be illuminated by the light of this divine Sun than by her own intelligence, which is only subject to error and illusion.

VIII

*Our Lord's infinite desire to be
united to souls in Holy Communion*

Desiderio desideravi hoc Pascha manducare vobiscum antequam patiar. "I have desired with a great desire," said our gracious Savior, "to eat this Passover with you before I suffer."[31]

There is a wonderful and very profound mystery to be discovered in this about the souls which Jesus fully possesses, but I am not worthy to explain it. I limit myself to the desires of Jesus, astonished at seeing a God capable of desires. Desires are the sign of the lack of something, so how is it possible that the Son of God can have desires, seeing that He is an infinite fullness and that He alone can satisfy all desires? This One, is He in need, who gives all the Blessed complete happiness and perfectly fulfills their desires? O ineffable love, which renders Jesus capable of desires and makes Him sigh, and drives Him with divine ardor to say, *"Desiderio desideravi!"*

What! My adorable Savior, how can You have desires? Are You not sufficient to satisfy Yourself with Your greatness and Your adorable perfections, with Your divine Father and the Holy Spirit? You who are the beatitude of all the saints and have had eternal joys before the world was made? My divine Savior, I perceive that since You have made your precious Body into a Eucharistic Bread, You can no longer be without desires, and consequently, without making it seem that something is lacking for the satisfaction of Your heart.

[31] Luke 22:15.

57

This infinite ardor (if I may speak of it this way) made You desire union with men through this mystery, which love instituted, in order to draw them to share in all that You are in Yourself. It is true that You are annihilated in the mystery of the Incarnation. What? That was not enough to satisfy You? No, Your love was not content; it wants to be annihilated in each soul in particular. *Desiderio desideravi.*

He wants to be eaten by us in order to establish His divine life in us, and that through this holy eating of His adorable Body we enter into Him and He into us, so that we become one with Him and He with us; and by this means to communicate to us all that He is as God, to the point of raising us to share in the divine nature: *Divinae consortae naturae.*[32]

Jesus Christ in the Most Holy Sacrament keeps this desire; He is still not satisfied. He will say unto the end of the ages, "*Desiderio desideravi.*" As long as there is a soul on earth capable of receiving His grace, He will have an infinite desire to draw her to His love, so that He might eat with her the Eucharistic Pasch. Oh! If we could comprehend the ardor of Jesus, we would swoon in amazement, seeing the vehemence of His divine charity. It is not that He needs us for the glory of His Father, but that He loves us in truth. He did not prize His blessedness if we had no share in it; because He looks upon us as members of His mystical Body, He cannot be satisfied if we were not united to Him and transformed into Him. Seeing us from His Eucharistic throne, He cries out to us, "*Desiderio desideravi.*"

Let us hasten then, my Sisters, let us hasten to the Blessed Sacrament! Let us go in order to satisfy the infinite desires of that adorable Heart. Let us receive Communion in order to

---

[32] 2 Peter 1:4.

please Him and to satisfy His infinite desires. Let us cast ourselves unconditionally at His sacred feet, saying to Him with reciprocal love, the most fervent possible for us, "O divine Heart! O loveable Heart! O Heart whose excellence and kindness are beyond words, satisfy Your desires in me. Draw me completely to You to satisfy Your desires. Be fed in Your own manner so that I may be Your substance, and that Your desires may be entirely satisfied. Communicate to my soul a small share of Your most ardent desire so that I may say with the same heart and the same love, through the pouring out of Your sacred desires in me, in Communion every day, *'Desiderio desideravi.'*"

IX

The solitude and silence Our Lord kept in the womb of His Holy Mother, and the extreme humiliations to which He is reduced in the Holy Eucharist

MY SISTERS, I think it would be more useful to remain in solitude and silence to hear the voice of God, and also more advantageous for the soul to speak *to* God rather than to speak *of* God. But since I am obliged to speak, I will tell you, my Sisters, that silence is a very holy thing. If I consider Jesus in the virginal womb of His glorious Mother, I find Him keeping a profound silence. The eternal Word became mute to give us esteem for silence and so that we might understand something of its greatness, since God, who can only say most excellent things, has come to earth to keep a prodigious silence. The holy Virgin will honor that sacred silence, speaking to no one about the divine mystery worked in her, and although she made haste to visit her cousin, as the evangelist says, it was without harming silence. We hear that she uttered at that time only a single word, the holy canticle of the *Magnificat*, which the Holy Spirit spoke through her mouth. And the presence of Jesus, hidden in the womb of His most pure Mother, sanctified St. John the Baptist, but without breaking the silence; everything was effected in a divine manner while they were in the wombs of their mothers. Consider this profound solitude! St. John leaping for joy and already transported with love towards his Savior, kept his mother in admiration and silence, so that she said only these brief

61

words, "*Unde hoc mihi*, etc."[33] Therefore, it is not a multitude of words which produces grace's good effects in the soul. Silence is the best disposition we can have to receive the impression of the divine mysteries, and especially that of the Incarnation, where all was done in silence, in the middle of the night.

Jesus and Mary say nothing. Do you not believe, my Sisters, that our blessed father St. Benedict had the intention of honoring their silence and solitude when he hid in the cave at Subiaco? Is it not his silence which produced the marvels of his order? God prepared him to receive the sublime effects of grace we see in him. In that dear solitude he was filled with the spirit of all the just and learned heavenly secrets which cannot be expressed by our words. The saints have always longed for solitude and silence and when these were torn away, they have borne this privation as a burden which was only tolerable by the sacrifice which they were making to the divine will. They knew by experience that the soul has difficulty keeping its purity and holiness apart from solitude, so they went back to it as soon as business or the command of God gave them the freedom to do so. Oh! What marvels God works in a solitary soul which is withdrawn from the multiplicity of creatures! Let us make room, my Sisters, for the eternal Word who is in us at Holy Communion to be heard. But let us also adore the captivity of Jesus in us, a dreadful and terrible captivity, if I dare to say it, which He endures in our bosoms! Yes, my Sisters, I say that He suffers in us, for though He is truly impassible and glorious in Himself, nevertheless He is like a prisoner and powerless in us, when we refuse Him absolute sovereignty over our hearts; we lodge Him in a dun-

---

[33] "And whence is this to me, that the mother of my Lord should come to me?" Luke 1:43.

geon darkened by our passions, our pride, and the thousands of other imperfections which darken the sky of our soul and make a dreadful prison for Jesus, in which He bears an appalling humiliation. Is there anything more outrageous?

Love makes Jesus descend into us to be our life and our light; and we reduce Him to a kind of powerlessness for producing His effects in us. My Sisters, the Church says with regard to the Holy Virgin: *Non horruisti virginis uterum.*[34] Oh! What should she say about us? The body of the most holy Virgin was a prison and seclusion for Jesus, it is true, but very different is the prison in our hearts, which are true dungeons, full of darkness and pollution. While Jesus was hidden in Mary, He suffered nothing from this captivity on her account; however, it must be agreed that, though she was more pure than the angels, it was an abasement for Jesus to abide there. But we say that He found there not captivity but an agreeable liberty, not a dark dungeon but a palace wholly brilliant with glory. In His most worthy Mother, Jesus was captive with respect to His divine person; but hidden in her virginal womb, He was perfectly free in His operations. He was in a dark prison outwardly, but otherwise all was brilliant with light, since Jesus, like a divine sun, was in the heaven of Mary's soul, where there had never appeared the slightest darkening of imperfection. Never had it been touched by the corruption of sin, but it was always sweet and delightful, giving joy to the heart of Jesus, who found in the womb of His Mother more happiness, more joy, and more pleasure than in the company of the angels in paradise. Thus, Jesus was free there; He was there without cloud and without any darkness. Mary received the fullness of this divine sun who worked in her without any resistance and with a wonderful sweetness.

---

[34] From the *Te Deum*, "Thou didst not abhor the Virgin's womb."

Oh my Sisters! It is not the same in our souls, which ordinarily cause obstacles to His rays and obscure His brilliance. And this, even to the extent of, in some way, interrupting God's omnipotence, which, with a single *fiat*, brought all things from nothing and which all inanimate, vegetative, and sensitive creatures obey, doing exactly what He created them to do. Oh, how often I have envied their happiness! They can say, "We came forth from God, we exist in God, never acting contrary to His divine will." O happy creatures, which always do what God wills and never depart from it for a single moment! It is only man, my Sisters, for whom God seems to have an infinite love, who pulls away, and draws back constantly from obedience. We know too well by our own experience that, since the sin of the first man, all his children have rebelled against God. Sin caused this disorder in us, giving us inclinations which are totally contrary to God's law. Our whole being remains tainted and corrupted by this, no rational creature [on earth] was exempted from this evil. My Sisters, I ask you, who among us can say like the plants, "I always abide in God; I always do what pleases Him"? Can anyone be found who remained faithful since the day of baptism or even since the day of religious profession? Alas! Not one. August Mother of my God, it is only you who can say it in truth.

My Sisters, let us continue to speak about the humiliations which Jesus has in us, in our Communions. How much we should be moved, on our own account and on account of the many people who receive Communion unworthily, and cause Jesus to suffer such terrible shame and insults! My Sisters, we who have the glory of being the Daughters and the victims of the Most Holy Sacrament, have we not good reason to weep? (I am not here speaking of the external profanations committed by the wicked, the account of which alone is enough to make one die of sorrow and fear.) Sacrilegious Communions, only too frequent among Christians, should they not over-whelm us with shock? Oh! Who can understand what injury the Son of God sustains from such Communions? I can say nothing to express such a deadly evil. It is the heart of all evils, since in a way Jesus receives a kind of death more shameful and cruel than that of His Passion. This evil is so terrible in its reality that it exceeds all human thoughts. It would be neces-sary to understand something of the infinite dignity, holiness, and greatness of God speak of it properly. I am quite certain, my Sisters, that none of us would wish to fall into this disor-der. I tell you this only to make you wonder at the excessive humiliations of God when He became man, and what He is subjected to in order to come into our hearts through Holy Communion. Also I know that you would not voluntarily allow a venial sin to enter your hearts and that you would rather descend into hell than insult your Spouse in this way; for if we were in that infernal abyss, God would not lose any of His glory. But to offend His Majesty in us by mortal sin is the only evil on earth which a soul should fear.

I want also to say a word to you about faults and lighter imperfections, my Sisters. I include the lesser ones, voluntary or from habit, which make Jesus Christ suffer a very great humiliation in us. Let us do all that we can to correct our-selves. And when we do not have any actual sins, have we not still an abominable depth in us? It is for Jesus an extreme humiliation to descend into that corruption. O divine purity! What humiliations You suffer! The angels are not pure enough in Your eyes, and we dare to come before You and receive You into our own pollution. O love! O love! You were not ignorant of this when You submitted to this Sacrament and com-manded us to receive You through It. O incomparable abase-ment of God! O Mystery of the Incarnation, perfectly completed by Communion! It was not enough for You to become flesh in the womb of a most pure Virgin, You had to be annihilated in us in order to suffer there extreme humiliations and lose Your sacramental Being by which You expend yourself in homage to the infinite being of God Your Father. And by this eating we are transformed into You in a way so exalted and so sublime that all the theology and eloquence of men cannot explain it. What! Jesus comes into us to repair the disorder which sin incessantly causes in us. He comes to glorify His Father by the greatest humiliation that He could have on earth. O profound abasement, which gives to the Father a glory and infinite delight! My soul, you cannot abase yourself enough before the Majesty of God, as much as He deserves, and so Jesus comes to make up for your lack; through His annihilation in you, He gives an honor and an exaltation to God which is divinely infinite. He comes to continue His life: humiliated, poor, abject, penitent, and sorrowful.

Oh! My Sisters, can we not appreciate a little the benefits this grace of Jesus gives us through the Holy Eucharist! Let us have more love than ever for Holy Communion, be more faithful, and try to make a better use of it. Let us be solitary with Him in our hearts, not leaving Him alone in us, occupying ourselves only with Him, freeing ourselves from many mistakes, from vain curiosity, from hastiness, and so on. For, though all of this may be involuntary, it always creates some obscurity [in our souls]. At the very least, we should humble ourselves in His holy presence under the weight of our misery, remaining at His feet with meekness and tranquility of spirit, not caring for any earthly thing. A servant of God said that a soul in the presence of God should be so detached from creatures that if the world were to come to an end, the soul should not even turn her head to view the ruin, so much should she regard all things as nothing compared with God!

X

The birth of Our Lord and the profound humiliations He endures in the Blessed Sacrament

I CANNOT ENTER into the solemnity of this holy day without inviting you to come to adore greatness humbled, power become weakness, infinite majesty reduced to nothing, eternal Wisdom become a babe, immensity in miniature, and the Holy of Holies, the one whom the seraphim extol as thrice holy, reduced to the likeness of a sinner, and as St. Paul says, made sin,[35] in order to become the victim for sinners. Here, come to earth, is the pure victim, the holy victim, the spotless victim.[36] This is the day on which God enters into power over God, the day on which God sees Himself adored by God, and on which God is sacrificed to God. O day full of mysteries, marvels, and wonders! Day which caused the Angels' admiration and which completes the joy of the eternal Father! All the divine attributes receive a new glory on this day. God becomes a Child. *Verbum caro factum est.* God's holiness is revered with perfect worship. This is a perfection in God which is inaccessible [to us], but it is He Himself who adores it in fullness. This is the day of the first adoration worthy of God; if on this day God is annihilated, it also the day of His triumph, since He becomes the prey and victim of justice.

Oh holy day! Oh glorious day! Oh sacred moment, in

[35] 2 Corinthians 5:21.
[36] From the Roman Canon.

which Jesus becomes a babe and in which the august Trinity receives from Him an infinite glory and delight. Oh day of love! Oh day of joy! *Gaudium magnum.* Oh day of blessing and glory. *Gloria in excelsis Deo.* Oh day so ardently desired, which restores the reign and kingdom of God over all mankind. Day beyond description because of its excellence, but which we should bless and love with all our hearts, since it re-establishes us in peace: *Et in terra pax hominibus bonae voluntatis.* The causes of our jubilation are the humiliations, poverty, contempt, sufferings, annihilations, and death of a God. Jesus comes into the world, in our flesh, to be the victim of the divine justice and holiness. He comes to be sacrificed and to lose His life, and this is our joy. Oh depth! Oh abyss full of mysteries! The miseries, the pains, the poverty, the humiliations of a God, all this causes our felicity. Yes, this is the happiness and hope of our eternal destiny; for it is by being born, suffering, and dying that He begins to reconcile us with His Father. Since we receive such great benefits from the Child-God, let us go to pay Him homage; let us go to gaze upon Him in the stable, on the straw where He makes His first sacrifice in the capacity of victim. Oh Jesus, Child-God! As soon as You appear on earth, You are destined to die, You breathe only sacrifice; and the love that drew You from the bosom of Your Father brings You to the Cross and to death. This was the first act You made on coming into the world, immolating Yourself to give an infinite glory and honor to Your Father, and to make reparation for the insults He received through the sins of men. Oh Jesus! From this moment we should regard You as a host. You came to die, and by dying You give us life. Grant us the grace that the moment of Your birth may be the moment of our death; that Your life alone may be our life. We ask You, Lord, to annihilate our life, so that we may have no other life than Yours.

That is what He desires of us, my Sisters. Therefore, let us cease to live. But how? Let us stop pursuing our own interests, following our humors, loving vanity and creatures. Let us stop being submerged in our senses, acting as if we were self-sufficient. God becomes a child for us to teach us littleness, simplicity, docility, surrender, abandonment, poverty, and so on. Let us bring to Him our poverty, our weaknesses, our darkness, our infirmities, our ignorance, our afflictions, our temptations, our sufferings, our abjection. All of this will be pleasing to Him; a child receives everything given to him. He does not expect heavenly gifts from us. He knows that we are in the world of sinners, which only brings forth thorns and thistles. It is pride for us to want to give Him what we do not have. He came to clothe Himself in our miseries and to bear our sorrows, as it says in the Prophet;[37] since He came to take these on Himself, can we give Him anything else? Let us stay at His feet, adoring Him along with His most holy Mother, and offer Him our poverty; provided we give it to Him gladly, He will be content. In exchange, He will give us the graces, virtues, and mercies contained in His littleness. Let us not leave Him, let us gaze at Him ceaselessly; and if we have no other way to honor Him than to behold Him, He will be very pleased with that, and our souls will be strengthened from it. Oh! The lovely gaze of the Child-God! A look of love, of sweetness, and of goodness. Let us be certain that He looks back at us, and that our hearts will not be long in His presence before they are wounded with a holy tenderness for this divine object of love.

A great saint exclaims with marvelous amazement, "Oh wondrous miracle, to see a God become an infant!" It is true, this can overwhelm men and angels with astonishment.

---

[37] Isaiah 53:4.

Because when I see God contained in a manger, and reduced to nothing in a manner so indescribable, I can only cry out, "Oh marvels! Oh prodigy! Oh abyss! Oh angels! Oh men! Oh, hell itself, be seized with astonishment!"

However, when I consider Him in the hearts of sinners—a detestable lodging, a million times worse than the stable of Bethlehem! He is contained there with the cruelest enemies who only plot His death, who trample Him under foot, and cause Him more shame than the poverty and discomforts of the stable. Moreover—frightful prodigy, which not only shocks us, but would make us die of horror—to see God in the hands of wicked and abominable sorcerers, put to use in some way for their diabolical malice. What! My God reduced to a condition so shameful, who remains in the Sacred Host, used as a charm and a spell? Could we not die merely from speaking of this horror? Oh God, who can understand it? What! The one who created heaven and earth, who punishes the rebel angels and faithless men with eternal torment, who causes the whole world to tremble when it pleases Him to make the blows of His power and justice felt, the One who drew all things from nothing and who by His will alone could return them to it—He becomes a nothing Himself!

In this divine Sacrament He surrenders His strength, His glory, and His power. Does it not seem that He has become powerless, by allowing Himself to be taken and carried by sacrilegious and vile hands, who touch Him only to profane Him, and if they could, to tear away from Him His being and life? Oh! With what rage those wretches treat the love of my divine Master, which makes Him like a prisoner in the Tabernacles, to exercise a tyrannical power over His divine Person for their abominable schemes! Oh marvel! Oh prodigy! I would like to exclaim it through the whole world! There is nothing so shocking! A God in the hands of demons, a God who endures things I cannot say.

The birth of Our Lord; His profound humiliations

Oh, how happy are those souls who, through divine wisdom's dispensation, through the secret of His divine counsels, are subjected to the power of this evil darkness, of those wicked devils, whether by sorcery or other means—they are happy in suffering their dreadful tyranny, if they choose to endure faithfully this sorrowful state in homage to the one the Son of God bears for His Father in the mystery we adore. Since He is present in the Eucharist in His many mysteries, I think there are souls destined to render Him homage in each one of the states found there, and in each humiliation that He received there; and according to the experience of His ways in souls, it seems clear that some are particularly called and chosen to honor His incomprehensible abjection and humiliations. Oh! What graces they receive in this state, although unknown by them, if they unite themselves to Jesus' state in the hands of the impious. They should do so, and He desires it of their fidelity. He desires adorers for all His states, as we already said, and also participates in them. Now, is there anything more just than to render Him homage in the state of which we are speaking, since He suffers more humiliation in it than in any other of His most holy life? We adored this divine Savior in the hands of demons in the desert during His forty days of penance, when He was carried through the air, and gave His holy humanity into their power, and was transported to the pinnacle of the Temple, and onto the mountains. Why do you think He gave them this permission? Oh mystery unheard of! It was to console and sustain the souls who were destined to extreme pains and temptations, so that they are not surprised if they experienced the fury of those cruel tyrants who, not being able to destroy and annihilate Jesus Christ, have an implacable rage against the souls who bear His likeness through holy baptism, and who are destined for heaven. It is true that this condition of the desert should

71

cause great wonder, seeing God in such humiliation; but I say gladly that this is little in comparison to what He endures in the adorable Eucharist, and that the shameful uses to which He is put are inconceivably more humiliating.

XI

The life hidden in Jesus Christ

IT IS TRUE, my Sisters, and you are not ignorant of it, that your profession obliges you to live henceforth in a state of continual death. You swore a solemn and irrevocable oath about this; from that obligation there is no appeal or dispensation. You are subject to the sentence which St. Paul declares on behalf of God: "You are dead and your life is hidden with Jesus Christ in God."[38] If your life is buried in Jesus, you should no longer appear to have any sign of life. Jesus alone should appear, because in truth He is the only life, and the wellspring of all life. It would be an affront to this source of life, an insupportable injury which would earn infinite punishments, to hinder the divine life even for a moment; it would be better to descend into hell than to stop it for an instant. Given this, it is a question of knowing how your soul should remain hidden, entirely buried in Jesus Christ, and how to live this life of death. Sisters, I am not capable of speaking about this state; I will merely say, to fulfill my obligation, that you must bring a spirit of annihilation in all things and in all places; without choice, without desires, without affections, without plans, and having no other will than to be uniquely Jesus Christ's. And this, without [independent] action, without haste, without worry, and without the impetuosity of your own mind, having constantly in the depth of your heart an inclination, an overflow, and a loving possession

[38] Colossians 3:3.

73

of Jesus in you. And this, through a disposition of pure faith, thus allowing yourself to be lost in Him, like a little stream which empties into the ocean, allowing yourself to be buried and completely swallowed up without any recourse. Being lost in this way, your own interests will also be lost and nothing created will be able to draw you away from this blessed center. Then you are dead, since Jesus alone is living.

A continual gaze at your nothingness will keep you in this death very easily, if you faithfully follow the attraction which is felt in the depth of your soul. Living thus, you may say that you do not live at all. Oh, blessed death which gives life to Jesus! Never is He so glorious in us, whatever love we feel for Him, than when we make Him live in this way; the soul in this state has everything and endures everything. Jesus alone lives in her and He is everything and He suffices for everything to die continually.

This state of perpetual death should be resolved into some simple practices which can help the soul remain there continually. I pray that Our Lord will give light to someone to lay out a system along these lines. For those whom God has called there, I only say that you must make frequent use of recollection, not only to silence your lower nature, but [to enter] a silence of the spirit: first, with regard to self and creatures; second, abandon all your interests to Jesus Christ, handing over everything which concerns you to His gracious providence; third, exactness in all your observances; fourth, never do anything according to your own judgment; fifth, never allow yourself or others anything that is not for the glory of God. (This is a delicate point, as nature is often found covering itself with the interests of God.) Sixth, do not keep anything created in your mind, unless charity for your neighbor or obedience requires it for the fulfillment of your duties. Seventh, remain peaceful and never let yourself be preoccupied about anything which would disturb your soul in the least. Eighth, cherish all occasions to sacrifice yourself to Our Lord, every cross and contradiction sent by Providence; do not attempt to justify yourself unless you are forced to do so; die with Jesus Christ always. Ninth, when those whom God put in authority over you ask about the state of your soul, your sufferings, and so on, be very simple. Tenth, your senses are also animated not by God's grace but with a natural life that leads them to sin; they are still living their natural life. I do not know if you understand me.

XII

God keeps the soul in a state of death before giving it His divine life

OH! What an unfathomable mystery! There is nothing more astonishing, all seems lost. Nothing, nothing, nothing, nothing, nothing everywhere! Such nakedness is so great that it is surprising the soul can bear it. If it was perceptible, the soul would die of sorrow, but she can neither move, nor desire, nor will anything. All seems dead, and all waits for the breath of Jesus Christ. It is impossible for the soul to have in its power or its capacity a breath of life: these are the perpetually dead who await their resurrection from the pure power and mercy of Jesus Christ, without the soul being able to contribute the smallest thing. The soul sees this death clearly, though sometimes a mist covers it; sometimes she is completely dead and other times she can be disturbed, but although she may have different dispositions, death is always in the ground [of the soul].

Here there is something like a grain of wheat which falls to the earth; it dies, it decays, but in the depth of its own corruption there is a vegetative life which is preserved and which is not perceived because the grain seems to perish. This vegetative life is a productive power which is found in all plants and gives them life.

It is also like this in a soul which is dead and seems completely decayed and engulfed by its own corruption. I am not talking about souls dead because of sin, but of those of whom it is said in Scripture: "*Beati mortui qui in Domino moriun-*

77

tur."[39] The soul is dead, she no longer has life; but she perishes further, she decays more, and consequently seems diseased and finds herself unbearable. But, O marvelous secret, which I see as clear as day! In the depth of that death and decay, there is a seed of life which we can call a ground of life. In fact, it is not by virtue of the soul, or something which could come from [her] production or capacity, but by pure divine mercy. And this seed or ground of life is nothing other than Jesus Christ. It is not a grace or a share in some favor. We must say that it is Jesus Christ Himself who is in this wretched ground as life and as the center of life, but essentially life. I cannot express it in any other way, because there are no words to say better what I understand. I will say willingly something which would surprise many: that as the grain of wheat does not contribute to its rebirth, or its new life, but only remains in the earth and decays, in the same way, the soul also should remain buried in the earth of its own nothingness and its own corruption, awaiting with an eternal patience (that is, a miraculous patience) the moment of her resurrection. For, this seed of life hidden in the soul, without her discerning it at that time, cannot lose its life in that dirt or that corruption, because it is life, *Ego sum vita*,[40] and essentially life. If the soul does not suffocate or tear out this precious seed of life by sin, it will grow and produce a wonderful rebirth in the soul. But we must notice that the grain of wheat remains decayed in the earth and that it did not have its own seed which was fruitful. Just so, the soul the remains as one buried, decayed, and lost in the earth of her nothingness. It is Jesus Christ who grows and brings forth ineffable things in the soul, things which cannot be described. Accordingly, the soul must remain always in a state of death

---

[39] "Blessed are the dead, who die in the Lord." Revelation 14:13.

[40] "I am the way, [and the truth and the life.]" John 14:6.

until she passes into Jesus Christ as into the source of life, waiting for Him to produce Himself in her as life. The grain of wheat is the comparison which the Son of God gave us in the gospel and which He applied to Himself.[41]

Therefore, there is nothing to do in this state, my Sisters, except to suffer death and its corruption. Here is the whole secret of the interior life, which has so occupied minds, and which so many books discuss (which very often produce little light and little fruit, burdening souls with thousands of exercises or human thoughts which distance souls from the simplicity of Jesus Christ). I believe that a soul does well, when she can, to adore Jesus Christ as life in her, as her true life, and as the center of her life. She should bask in this divine Sun so that He warms this earth and after this she will produce results which conform to their principle. The soul can use the words of the Church, "*Rorate caeli desuper,*" and "*Aperiatur terra et germinet salvatorem.*"[42] I say this for those who are not yet in total ruin and dead to themselves. But when the soul is buried in her corruption there is no rule to give her, all depends on the pure kindness and mercy of Jesus Christ. The soul no longer has any power, any desires, any fervor, any plans, any inclinations, any will, any expectations, any movements. If I dare to say so, everything seems reduced to death. If it pleases Jesus Christ to do in that soul what His divine Spirit did in the vision of the prophet when He breathed on those dead bones and each one was animated with new life:[43] in the same way, if it pleases Him to breathe and to produce Himself in the soul, since He is life in truth, then this soul

---

[41] John 12:24.

[42] "Drop down dew, ye heavens . . . let the earth be opened, and bud forth a saviour." Isaiah 45:8.

[43] Ezekiel 37:3.

will be happily resurrected. But she must not long for her resurrection; it is the work of God's omnipotence to resurrect the dead. Thus, it will be the pure goodness and mercy of Jesus Christ which will bring it about when and how it pleases Him, without the soul being able to contribute the slightest breath, except for not preventing it, remaining faithfully in death. Here is all that she can do, for there is nothing in her power to effect or to hasten this resurrection.

Many times I have thought that these words of the gospel, "*In patientia vestra [possidebitis animas vestras]*,"[44] apply to this death. It requires a terrible patience because this resurrection depends on the pure mercy of God, and it pleases Him sometimes to postpone it such a long time that the soul almost loses hope of ever receiving it. I think in certain persons it only happens through bodily death, by an admirable wisdom which is beyond conception. For the good of these souls He keeps them in these dark prisons, or else they would be lost. If they perceived that great day, this Sun in its brilliance, in its eternal splendor, would make them blind; they could not bear it, being so weak. It is true that there are souls who are in this state of death for long years; this happens sometimes because death is not completely finished, but is only an apparent death in some way and not total. And as nature is dreadful in its own life, having a cunning which is almost infinite, it must suffer assaults and battles for a long time before its power is destroyed. I wish that each soul who, by the grace of Our Lord, feels in herself this law of death, would bear "patience" engraved on her heart and on her arm.[45] The need of this is so great that, if I said it for entire years, I would not be believed.

---

[44] "In your patience you shall possess your souls." Luke 21:19.
[45] Cf. Song 8:6.

Concerning the divine life which Jesus Christ reproduces in souls thus dead and decayed, it happens to the degree that it pleases Him to manifest Himself, to some more, to others less, but the little that He gives her is always excessive and infinitely more than the soul would dare to hope; for those moments, as the tiniest parts of this life, are so precious that we ought to suffer all imaginable martyrdoms to have the grace to possess even the smallest bit which Our Lord wished to give. But know that it is always the gift of God, and bought only with death; there is no currency on earth equal to its price and value. Let us remain then in this absolute necessity of death, let us die night and day, and on every occasion, but still more within ourselves, where our own life finds its support in a strange way.

XIII

The soul's abandonment to God's good pleasure

ALL OUR DESIRES must be limited by love of God's good pleasure; we desire Him to reign over us with the completeness with which He reigns in Heaven. May all our delight be that "God is the one Who Is," that He alone should *be*, and everything else annihilated. A real Christian, one who does not live for his own interests, is living completely in love and for love. All his pleasure is that God is content, that He is glorious, that He reigns, that He is loved. My Sisters, this is what should most occupy your souls, not allowing them to live for themselves, or to reflect on their paths in order to complain about the acts of divine Providence, or lower themselves to the level of the senses to satisfy self-love. We must not live as in times past but walk in newness of life, as St. Paul says.[46] We must live the new life of Jesus Christ, a life of grace, a life of faith, which separates us from life in ourselves, which is completely contrary to the life of Our Lord Jesus Christ.

The first step is abandonment. This is done by the complete resignation of oneself, relinquishing oneself entirely to the power and virtue of Jesus Christ, sacrificing oneself to all the eternal designs of God and resolving to live henceforth in this pure and holy abandonment which gives the soul entirely to Jesus Christ. Take note, therefore, my Sisters, as the first step that you leave yourself and your own actions to enter

[46] Romans 6:3.

into Jesus Christ and live only for Him. Thus, you are no longer your own, you have no rights over yourself and all you do for yourself is stolen from Our Lord Jesus Christ. You must remain totally abandoned to the divine disposition for time and for eternity. Do not worry about your own interests, but only abide in faith under God's guidance, with a confidence full of love, always walking the road which holy Providence gives you. Have for every different circumstance only a simple and humble submission to God's good pleasure, a simple acquiescence to His adorable guidance, finding good whatever He does with you since all His work pleases Him, without examining either yourself, what you are, or what you are becoming, but content in your simple and loving abandonment. Take pleasure only in the fact that God is in you and that He is as He wishes, doing His work in destroying yours, killing your self-love, and giving you matter for suffering and sacrifice. Happy and a thousand times happy is the soul who loves God for God alone and who loves Him more than her own life! My Sisters, loving Him more than your own life means loving Him beyond your feelings, loving without self-interest, loving His actions and His ways which bring us to annihilation. In a word, loving Him for Himself means losing oneself in His good pleasure. Let us love Him this way, and someday we will taste His divine sweetness, since after we have been purified like gold in the crucible, He will make us worthy to be perfected in His love, but we must suffer extraordinarily before rejoicing in that grace.

O my God! Why do worldly persons have more desire for vanities than we have to become worthy of Your love? They wear themselves out with pleasure and relentlessly seek worldly things but we do not want to suffer anything for the sake of God and the establishment of His kingdom! His ways seem harsh to us, and we complain about our darkness, our powerlessness, our hardness, and under the pretext of the love of God, we will not bear our miseries. We are like blind men, we do not see that our self-love and our secret pride do not want to be destroyed and do not want to feel the weight of humiliation. However, a soul properly abandoned to God allows herself to be consumed by His good pleasure. This soul knows that God's ways are holy and she submits humbly and confidently to His plans, pleased to be annihilated. Knowing she deserves eternal damnation, she adores His justice and mercy, resigning herself entirely and without reservation to the divine disposition. She prefers to be in darkness, in poverty, in misery, and in want, by order of God's good pleasure, than to be full of light and love through her own will.

Secondly, you must walk by faith, for if you are not equipped with the shield of faith you will remain neither firm nor steady in the ways of grace. When nature, the feelings, and human ways of thinking have been destroyed, faith alone should support the soul. Therefore, live by faith, my Sisters, work by faith, love and suffer in faith, since through this virtue you will be detached from your senses and live a purer life. This is what you must do, and learn how to submit to God, but without keeping anything back. There are many souls who work toward perfection, but very few are successful, because they seek themselves too much. Perfection consists in being so united to God's good pleasure that we become one with Him by the transformation of our will in His. It is a purgatory for souls who are little abandoned and do not want lose themselves to give life to Jesus. Do not be one of those, my Sisters; leave yourselves entirely to God. Remain in your nothingness before His holy presence and give Him the freedom to do in you and with you whatever will please Him.

Perfection does not consist in our operations; it is not something of us, but Jesus Christ, for us. It belongs to Him to cause it by pouring Himself out on our souls, since He alone is perfection. And when the soul is abandoned wholly to Him, surrendering herself, He establishes Himself there, He lives and reigns there: and that is perfection. Now, in this way the soul has nothing to do except to leave herself to God in a pure abandonment, without worrying about her defects, her miseries, and all the rest, since she cannot be better than she is. And thus she awaits in patience the coming of Jesus in her, to live His life and establish His kingdom.

XIV

The divine will

ABOUT THE DIVINE WILL, my Sisters, I can tell you nothing except that it is beyond description and that there is nothing which distinguishes it from God Himself. I do not feel capable of saying anything else, except that it is the Sovereign of heaven and earth, and its power is so great it extends even over God Himself. You see this in the adorable person of Jesus Christ, subject to the divine will from the first moment of His Incarnation and in all the rest of His life. Contemplate Him in the Garden of Olives, adoring and making fitting atonement[47] for our contempt and disobedience towards the divine will. See the depths to which He descends in order to exalt it: He is prostrate on the ground to demonstrate His submission.

---

[47] The reparation of honor (i.e., rather than pecuniary reparation) was used in France as a punishment from the fifteenth to the seventeenth century. It was a punishment inflicted, before execution, for every grave offense against God, the Church, the State, the public order. The condemned, in his shirt, candle in hand and rope around his neck, knelt before all, asking pardon.

Mother Mectilde adopted a similar symbolic ceremony for her monasteries, to signify the solidarity in sin which binds all men, and thus also the nuns to their brethren in the world, redeemed in a superabundant manner by solidarity in Christ (Romans 5:12–21).

"The reparation of honor made to the Blessed Sacrament, the candle in hand, is an act of humiliation, confessing we are criminals, but it can only be received by the Father through Jesus Christ." *Documents Historiques*, 123.

He knows the divine will was profaned by Adam and that all his posterity followed the evil tendency of that rebel. This is why Our Lord annihilates Himself before its greatness and renders it an infinite glory by giving it supremacy over His divine person. He goes further: He wants this divine will to be avenged for the contempt which men have shown it; and for this reason, He reduces Himself to such subjection that He makes Himself not only its slave, but bears the weight of its omnipotence by allowing Himself to be crushed.

Behold how great is the power of the divine will: it vanquishes God! In some way, it annihilated Him; it did its good pleasure by nailing Him to a cross, where He died in homage to that supreme will. See, my Sisters, the sovereignty exercised over God Himself. Consider its dominion over the Blessed in heaven; it constitutes their beatitude and arranges all the beautiful harmony of the heavens and is the delight of the saints; it constitutes their repose and orders the various degrees of their glory. It also makes God rule in our hearts. If I consider the economy of grace in the Church and in the souls of Christians, it is the divine will which governs it. There is no virtue apart from the divine will, no perfection or holiness, no joy or peace, no light or fervor. We must conclude, then, that all happiness is contained in the divine will and that only a soul which is possessed by it is happy, and enjoys, even in this world, a foretaste of Paradise. Everything good follows from it: [in it] there is no trouble or anxiety, no inconstancy or pretension, no eagerness or sadness, no fear or darkness; all is serene in the divine will, all is light and clarity, all is immovable. Since the divine will is God Himself, we must believe that a soul cannot be animated by it unless she is completely filled with God.

It would not be difficult to prove from Scripture and the Fathers that Our Lord Jesus Christ was the victim of the divine will, which He always adored, since He accomplished it perfectly at every moment of His holy life. Let us try to imitate Him and give ourselves today as slaves of love to the divine will so that it may regain its rights over us, and that henceforth we might act only according to its inspirations and suffer for its sole and unique pleasure.

Also let us reflect a little, my Sisters, concerning the designs of love and the goodness of the divine will towards us. How many favors and inspirations, how many occasions of grace has it given to us? We have neglected, despised, and often rejected it, preferring our own wicked and detestable wills to the divine will. We must make fitting reparation[48] and profess a new fidelity to it, giving it an absolute reign over us. And since we have been the slaves of our passions and our inclinations, we must submit absolutely to all its laws, so that it alone may live and reign in us.

---

[48] *Amende honorable.*

XV

The reign of Jesus Christ

GOD REQUIRES an absolute reign over souls; but He finds very few who agree to it. It consists of an abandonment of ourselves and a pure dependence on God, with a faithful renunciation of self, and a mortification of everything which might create obstacles to God's reign in the soul, down to the destruction of the smallest imperfection.

The majority of spiritual persons, even the most advanced, cause a great obstacle to the reign of God in themselves by too much curiosity. They give their minds the freedom to investigate the workings of God, seeking to understand things to which they should surrender their intellects, through submission and annihilation. Oh wretchedly miserable life, completely filled with sin, entirely opposed to God, and which destroys the reign and the glory of Jesus Christ! I have no words to say what I feel about this; I have a disgust too great to express—what use is so much discourse? Such things are for great souls who are full of God and illumined by His lights, who can speak with assurance about what they receive from His goodness.

My soul, let us keep a profound silence in all dispositions, and may everything in us be annihilated, not finding life in self or creatures. Let us allow everything to return to its source, and keep nothing for ourselves, and after having received many favors and graces, let us live as if we had not received them. Let us remain as if dead in a perfect detachment, irrevocably, without reflection, and as if without knowing the hand of God touches us to have mercy on us. Let us not find our life in the gifts of God or His lights. Our life should be animated by the good pleasure of God. He should be the soul of our soul; it is He who should give us life and cause us to act. Apart from this life there is no pure life in us, all is corrupt. Instead, we must lose and reduce to nothing what we are in ourselves, in creatures, and with respect to God's gifts. Before arriving at this annihilation we must lose these three things. Then, my soul, you will be nothing more than a pure capacity for God's good pleasure, who will do with you and in you what pleases Him. Oh! How good it is to be nothing and to count on nothing but God!

It is impossible to find God in seeking ourselves. We must walk in the darkness to find the light, lose ourselves to find ourselves, die in order to live, be annihilated so that God may reign. "Blessed are the poor in spirit for the kingdom of heaven is theirs."[49] What is this poverty of spirit? It is a soul stripped of creatures and herself. The Spirit of God is master of the soul who is abandoned to Him; He makes her poor. Why? Because God cannot rule in a soul which is filled and occupied with something [else]. The one who possesses something is not poor; but the one who dies continually to all sensible things, who endures the privation of all help, who is pleased even with the exterior exercise of poverty; who frees her mind of all creatures; who does not want to rest in any of them, however excellent they may be; the one who does not admit any thought of esteem for herself or praise from others; who, in a spirit of continual simplicity towards God has no other desire than Him alone; who desires to know nothing except Him; who seeks nothing outside of Him; who is not attached to His gifts and favors and does not appropriate any

---

[49] Matthew 5:3.

good to herself; who remains in her littleness and makes it her place of repose—that person can have full possession of the kingdom of God. According to the gospel, it is given only to the violent, since they alone carry it away who can overcome themselves and go beyond their senses and passions.[50]

Now, what is meant by the kingdom of God and how should it be understood? The kingdom of God in us is nothing other than God living and reigning in the soul who possesses Him, as in His heavenly Palace. He is master and sovereign there; He makes the laws and everything is subject to Him. The phrase 'kingdom of God' means that God alone occupies the whole soul; that nothing appears in her except Him; that she is so perfectly subject to Him in everything that her will disappears. The only thing remaining to her is the sole and unique desire to see God live in her more and more, up to the complete loss of herself in Him. This is her only longing, the only treasure which remains to her; and although she is still animated with this desire, it is in a manner so peaceful and gentle that this desire passes from God into her, and from her into God, continuing in this way without slackening, but always without agitation or anxiety.

Blessed is the soul who has this heavenly beatitude, who is poor in spirit through the Spirit of God Himself; the one whom grace has made poor and not the constraint of life's misfortunes. Let us love this precious poverty, let us choose it through the inspiration of the Holy Spirit and say, Oh holy poverty, which makes the reign of God Himself triumph in me! I choose you, and I want to welcome you into my heart. I want to give Jesus the joy of seeing His reign established there and that my heart is completely filled with Him. I no longer want creatures, plans, projects, desires, or affection for any

[50] Cf. Matthew 11:12.

created thing. I do not desire to possess anything. Oh, blessed poverty! Oh sacred indigence! Blessed be the day when I see in myself this perfect deprivation of all things, and seeing myself stripped of everything, I will be clothed with you, in you, and for you. Oh adorable Jesus! You are the only one who is truly poor and the only one in whom God ruled supreme, without any resistance!

Let us speak of Your poverty, oh my Savior! Alas! Who can comprehend it? A life poor, unknown, and suffering. A life of unfathomable privation: poor in the womb of His glorious Mother, poor in the manger, poor on the flight into Egypt, poor in the house of St. Joseph, poor in the desert of His penitence, poor in His public life, poor on the Cross, poor in His death, and prodigiously poor in His divine Eucharist! This extraordinary poverty gives an infinite glory to God His Father and makes Him reign fully. This same kingdom of God is ours, but only the one who is perfectly poor understands it. Those who do not have a pure heart will never possess it; it is shown only to the poor and the little, who are no longer anything in themselves, to those who are buried in littleness and nothingness. When everything in the soul is consumed in this way, then Jesus rises like a glorious sun in the sky of the soul (which is the deepest part of its mind and of its substance), and He sheds His divine rays, which fill the soul's interior completely, with glory, joy, love, and blessing beyond description.

XVI

We should form one body with Jesus Christ

I<small>T IS AN AMAZING THING</small> to know by faith that we form a single body with Our Lord Jesus Christ and that, despite this precious truth, we are almost never united to that adorable Head by attention and by continual application. As members, we have an ineffable kind of union [with Christ] and consequently a happiness, a grace, and a gift of infinite value. Nevertheless, my Sisters, we spend hours, days, weeks, and maybe even entire months without making a solid return, without reflecting on it, and without giving it credit.

I am lost in amazement which I cannot get over, and the more I speak about it, the more I wonder at it, and the more I see the wretchedness of a soul which remains trapped in its senses. O how great is this falsehood! We see created things with our eyes, we hear them with our ears, we touch and taste and all of it is nothingness, distraction, and illusion.

O God! Eternal truth, because we do not see You, because we do not sense You, because we do not touch You, we ignore what You are! Uncreated Being, existing in Yourself, all creatures exist only in You, and through You, and meanwhile, You seem to be distant from us because we do not live by the Faith which makes us believe what You are. Sense objects so fill our minds and our hearts that there seems to be no place to receive You. What misfortune! To live in God and yet not to live from God! Not believing in Him or making only feeble returns [to Him]!

To become a member of Jesus Christ, the Son of God, and

not to remain united to His Heart as that from which we continually receive life! If God is inaccessible because He abides in Himself and in His holiness, should we not become more intimate with the presence of His Son Jesus Christ, whom love has made ours, such that He took on our nature, in order to dwell with us? My soul, why do you so easily leave this loveable Jesus, in your thoughts and in the rapport of union and abandonment, though you form part of His Body? Can the arm stay alive if it is torn from its head? How can you live if you are separated from Jesus Christ? It is an absolute necessity to remain intimately united; apart from Him you have neither life nor action. It is from Him that you receive life at every hour and every beat of your heart. (I am here speaking of the life of grace and not of the physical life which we have in common with animals.) This divine life which Jesus grants us through Himself and which He so admirably imparts to us, though in a way beyond understanding, is the true life, from which we must live and which alone deserves the name of life.

I could give many reasons to demonstrate that it is the only life, but I omit all my thoughts in order to conclude: Jesus in the Most Holy Sacrament unceasingly breathes forth this precious life to us. This is why He dwells in the sacred ciborium, and why it is contained in the tabernacles on our altars.

Allow me to add that, renewing this mystery of love by the continual sacrifice which priests offer every day, we must communicate also for its perfect accomplishment, along with the priest who offers Our Lord and receives Him into his soul. When no one else receives Communion, we can say, in a certain way, that something is lacking to the sacrifice. Why? It is because, since Jesus instituted it in order to give us His life and transform us into Himself in a divine manner, we should form a single victim with Him, and a single victim of love. I believe we do not fulfill our obligations toward Jesus-made-Sacrament if we do not receive Communion. And because we often lack the ability or the dispositions to receive that infinite gift through sacramental Communion, we are obliged to make a spiritual communion, that is, by desire, by love, by union and by participation in the sacrifice along with the priest. And I say too, along with Jesus, because we form part of the Body which is sacrificed.

XVII

The esteem and reverence we should have for God

Oh! How I pity the blindness of souls who do not know God, who are weary and bored in His holy presence, who are not moved to reverence by His greatness. "*Pleni sunt caeli et terra,*" the heavens and earth are full of the majesty of His glory,[51] and we do not think about it at all. We do not give ourselves to this adorable plenitude in order to take part. What pains me especially, my Sisters, is that during the most precious time of our life, the one dedicated to prayer, our souls remain without attention, without reverence, without vigilance, and without love towards a Majesty so adorable. Alas! If we were before an earthly monarch, what would our attitude be? And for a God of such greatness, of infinite holiness and majesty, we do not have the fortitude to wait upon His divine presence for one hour with reverence.

If we knew the consequences of the ruin we bring about through our fault, we would weep tears of blood. But we are in darkness, our senses cast us into blindness. Let us wake our spirits by faith, which shows us the esteem we ought to have for God and should humble us before His greatness. The seraphim in heaven are so full of loving reverence that they veil their faces, unable to bear the weight of His Majesty; and all the blessed annihilate themselves in His divine Essence, to render Him the most profound respect. Why do we who are

---

[51] Isaiah 6:3.

99

on earth do less than these celestial spirits in heaven? Is it not the same God? Is it not the same Divinity? And since we have Him truly present in us, He who is in the blessed, on His throne of glory—why do we not pay our respects to Him just as all the heavenly host does?

I know that the turmoil of the present life makes us incapable of crying with the celestial choir, "*Sanctus, Sanctus, Sanctus,*"[52] without rest and without interruption; but at least for the time given to us for prayer in particular, let us be before God with the love and reverence of the seraphim who cry out in a profound silence, "*Sanctus, Sanctus, Sanctus.*" Let us be before God, say I, in a profound abasement; and if we do not see His greatness with the eyes of the body, we should see it purely and more truly with the eyes of the soul, by a simple conviction of faith. Alas! If a damned person had one hour of our time to be converted, what use would he make of it? Let us be confounded and brought down to the center of hell, since we are so unworthy of glorifying God.

---

[52] Isaiah 6:3; Revelation 4:8–9.

XVIII
The soul's resemblance to Jesus in the Host [53]

EACH SOUL has a relation, by state, to Jesus in the Host. We must ask Him to give us light to know which one is ours and to bind ourselves to it lovingly and steadily, although it may be very harsh or crucifying to nature. We should have courage, knowing that it is Jesus, annihilated in this divine Sacrament, who prepared this state for us, and bestows it upon us and merits the grace for us to make a holy use of it. But in order to understand this better, we should know something of these states He has in the Eucharist and how the soul participates in them.

1. *Jesus, under the appearance of the Host, has the character of a servant.* The soul who pays homage to this state should regard it an honor to serve and be the slave of God's holy ones and also of sinners since Jesus came to serve them in this Mystery, although His service is so little known. The soul should serve her neighbor with meekness and respect, without expecting any reward other than humiliation and rejection. These are the rewards of souls who, by the command of God, are slaves for the salvation of others.

PERFECT CHARITY

2. *Jesus is immolated and becomes the victim of sinners in the Host.* The soul who renders homage to this state should bear the harsh consequences of divine Justice, to the degree to

[53] See Appendix 1 for commentary on this chapter.

101

which Our Lord will be pleased to give it to her. She is not her own, but should be devoured and consumed. This phrase encompasses every kind of suffering from God, men, demons, and self, through the pure love which makes the soul along with Jesus a victim of those who profane the Eucharist.

CONTINUAL DEATH

3. *Jesus is silent in the Host.* The soul who renders homage to this state should keep a profound silence with respect to creatures and self, not polluting her tongue with the follies which vanity and self-love produce, since she has the honor to receive Jesus in His divine Sacrament. She should keep the same silence in her interior, with regard to God, by a humble reverence which makes her attentive to the words of life He speaks in her.

PERFECT SILENCE

4. *Jesus in the Host is as one exiled and banished from His fatherland.* The soul who gives homage to this state should live as a stranger on earth, because in fact, she is in a place of exile and banishment, to which sin has reduced her. This soul must, like Jesus, have no part in the inheritance of sinners. Instead, suffering poverty with respect to all created things insofar as this grace requires it and as obedience will authorize, she will long unceasingly for her dear fatherland and for the blessed return to God, from whom she departed in her creation.

PURE LOVE

5. *Jesus exiled in the Host is unknown.* The soul who renders homage to this state should live unknown by men as much as possible, generously avoiding all that could cause her to have the least eminence, regarding herself only as nothing, who deserves to be always ignored by God and man. She should

only be seen when compelled by obedience and from a completely pure charity.

PROFOUND LITTLENESS

6. *Jesus is contradicted and persecuted in the Host.* The soul who pays homage to this state must bear the contradictions of creatures, allowing herself to be condemned in all she does, so that nothing is acceptable to others, although she tries to please them according to her duty. She should be glad to have no support or help, to be accused of wrongdoing, seeing that Jesus endures injuries and persecutions all the time, in exchange for the infinite love which holds Him captive beneath the appearance of the Host.

INVINCIBLE PATIENCE

7. *Jesus is powerless in the Host.* The soul who honors this state should bear her own weaknesses, nakedness, and afflictions by submitting to God's command, who takes from her the power of delivering herself from these crucifying dispositions. Jesus wills to become powerless [in the Eucharist], in order to oblige the soul to bear with meekness and resignation her own powerlessness.

PERFECT SUBMISSION

8. *Jesus is neglected and forsaken in the Host.* The soul who desires to render homage to this state should love being neglected by creatures and even by God Himself. When He takes away His gifts and leaves the soul like a stranger, she should not be eager to attract attention or to occupy the thoughts of men, not even for a single moment. Since Jesus is forgotten, neglected, and abandoned, where else should the soul be who promised to honor and imitate Him?

FLIGHT FROM CREATURES

9. *Jesus is in a state of death in the Host.* The soul who honors this state must die at each instant of her life. Through this continual death she adores the continual death and the destruction of the sacramental Being of Jesus, which happens every day in the Sacrifice of the Mass. She must be faithful, without listening to the cries and complaints of nature, since she cannot render more glory to Jesus than in offering Him her life which is destroyed continually through this death.

DESTRUCTION OF ONE'S ENTIRE BEING

10. *Jesus is penitent in the Host.* The soul who renders homage to this state should be in continual humiliation for herself and for sinners. She should do everything in a spirit of penitence, since she gives herself as a pledge, along with Jesus penitent, for sinners and for those who profane the divine Host. She should be detached from all the satisfactions of life and at the same time be immolated, to appease divine Justice and draw its mercy to sinners.

PENITENCE IN A SPIRIT OF REPARATION

11. *Jesus is handed over to the power of His enemies in the Host.* The soul who desires to honor this state must be resolved to bear often the difficulties of trials, temptations, shame, and insults from men and from demons, since Jesus seems to have no power to protect Himself. He endures their insults for the glory of God His Father and for us to merit the grace to bear patiently the tyranny of our enemies whom we cannot vanquish.

PERPETUAL SUFFERING

12. *Jesus is abandoned to Providence in the Host.* The soul who pays homage to this state should be in a state of continual and complete abandonment to the pleasure of divine Providence;

it will treat her as it does Jesus. It allows the Host to fall to the ground, to be carried by the wind, and a thousand other sorts of abandonments, so that whether the soul is injured, trodden underfoot, exalted or despised, she remains in a holy indifference to all the commands of this adorable Providence.

COMPLETE ABANDONMENT

13. *Jesus endures contempt and mistreatment from sinners in the Host.* The soul who renders homage to this state must suffer all the most harsh actions of God: contempt, insults, and persecution from hell itself, without having any right to complain. She endures rejection, mistreatment from men, in a word, all that is harsh and painful, since our Savior in the Eucharist is prey to the malice of sin and sinners.

SUFFERING

14. *Jesus is poor in the Host.* The soul which renders homage to this state must be stripped of all created things, having neither land, nor house, nor lodging, nor goods, nor honor, nor friends, and, when God wills it, suffering the lack of interior light, gifts, and the taste of divine things, in order to conform to Jesus who is poor in the Host, who has no place at all. O prodigy! He does not seem to be there! He possesses nothing! He has no movement and depends entirely on the sacramental Species.

POVERTY

15. *Jesus is buried in the Host.* The soul who renders homage to this state should have no more part in all that happens on earth. She is no more and should no longer be seen; she has no will or preferences, all is buried with Jesus. Through a holy indifference, she endures everything; she does not resent the insults and offenses of creatures. She rests in Jesus, never

departing the gracious care He gives those who belong to Him.

SUPREME INDIFFERENCE

16. *Jesus is annihilated in the Host.* The soul who renders homage to this state should be annihilated in all circumstances and in all places. She remains before God as if in a double nothingness of sin which merits eternal rejection: first, with respect to creatures, willing to be treated as nothing, forgotten as if she did not exist, and scorned by the whole world, and other harsh treatments, which the nothingness of sin merits; second, with regard to self, believing herself to be nothing.

ANNIHILATION

17. *Jesus renders sovereign homage to the holiness of God in the Host.* The soul who would have a resemblance to this holy state is obliged to be detached from everything on earth; from creatures and from herself, from the slightest imperfections. She should exert herself to never allow anything that could sully her in the least, so that she may render fitting homage and have a likeness to the holy God. There must be nothing impure in the soul whom He unites to that divine attribute through this sacred Mystery.

PURITY OF LIFE

18. *Jesus is hidden under the appearance of the Host.* The soul who pays homage to Jesus hidden in this state must not be in herself or in creatures. She should be seen only in Jesus, doing what He does for the glory of His Father, without seeing herself, or even being aware of her state and disposition.

COMPLETE FORGETFULNESS OF SELF

19. *Jesus is a prisoner of love in the Host.* The soul who renders homage to this state should hide in the Tabernacle, depriving herself of the liberty of the interior and exterior senses, of satisfaction from created things and what might please the spirit, so as to have no other delight than to see herself captive and prisoner for love of Jesus, just as He is reduced to being in the Tabernacle as in a prison.

CAPTIVITY OF THE SENSES

20. *Jesus is solitary in the Host.* The soul who pays homage to the solitude of Jesus in this mystery should, similarly, separate herself from conversation with creatures, fleeing all occasions which would distract her such as news, curiosities, attachments, pleasures, and even her interior conversation about all that could distract the soul from the precious solitude she should have continually with God.

PROFOUND SOLITUDE

21. *Jesus-Host.* The soul who renders homage to this state should become a Host, through the two qualities which It has: whiteness and roundness. The first signifies innocence and purity. The second, forming a circle with Jesus as its center, to which the whole circumference should tend. The Host cannot be divided, it is for God alone; so too, the soul cannot divide herself, she should be uniquely and entirely Jesus's.

FIDELITY IN REFERRING ONE'S WHOLE SELF TO GOD

22. *Jesus is lost among the wicked in the Holy Eucharist.* The soul who renders homage to this state should be lost in the profound and incomprehensible ways of God in her regard. She should also be lost with respect to creatures, not to be found among them, or in herself. Jesus seems to be lost in the Host, when those devils incarnate cast it into places of infamy

and into the earth. O abyss! O depth! It cannot be understood, though the love of God fathoms it by a divine power.

COMPLETE LOSS OF SELF

23. *Jesus is obedient in the Host.* The soul who pays homage to this state should be submissive to God in all the events of life, the most painful and difficult to bear, constantly obedient, and without reasoning about the person who gives the commands, since Jesus obeys priests, although they are sometimes wicked, and they consecrate [the Host] for sacrilegious ends. Jesus is subject to their word in order to give us an example of perfect obedience.

BLIND OBEDIENCE

24. *Jesus is captive in the Host.* The soul who renders homage to this state must bear a captivity of heart and mind to all the laws of the divine guidance, whether it is to the Rule, to her Superiors, or to her neighbor. Jesus, captive by an infinite love, wants to dwell with us, even to the consummation of the ages, and to be in us under the species of bread and wine in the Most Holy Sacrament. O captivity of Jesus in the heart of sinners, where He is more a slave than one can imagine! Be captive, then, to the will of God and to your neighbor (when the latter can be done without sin).

COMPLETE CAPTIVITY OF SELF IN A SPIRIT OF SACRIFICE

XIX

The love of scorn and contempt in which
a victim of the Blessed Sacrament should live

WHAT IS PROPER to creatures and the inclinations of the Old Man is to be seen; what is proper to the grace of Jesus Christ is to hide and annihilate oneself. Self-love wants to be noticed and to do those things which will make us admired; the grace of the victims of the Most Holy Sacrament is to flee and to hide in littleness, contempt, and nothingness. Seeing her God annihilated, trampled underfoot, unknown and hidden, how would it seem for a victim to want to be esteemed and appear to be what she is not?

A victim should never seek praise, satisfaction, or her own justification when despised. A Daughter of the Most Holy Sacrament should not be acquainted with honor, glory, esteem, and eminence. She should never have more shame than when dragged from her nothingness, brought forward, and elevated. Her life is to be unknown, forgotten, and hidden from all creatures, as Jesus is in the Host; likewise, she cannot be recognized, and should endure the opposite only as an extreme crucifixion. What do you think it means to be a victim of the Most Holy Sacrament? It is to be a poor convict who expects nothing but death. The sentence of death was pronounced at the moment she became a victim. She has nothing more to do with creatures, her endowment is nothing but shame and insults and everything humiliating. The most painful cross of a victim is to be torn from her prison and be shown honor among men.

Therefore, we who have the grace to be the victims of Jesus should flee. Let us flee all the loftiness of earth; let us rejoice when others are praised, esteemed, and when they are on the throne of glory and exaltation. But let us weep tears of blood if we are so unfortunate as to have some consideration in men's thoughts. We must never leave our nothingness, to which Jesus annihilated in the Host has done us the honor of leading us. Let us flee the world, let us flee pomp, esteem, reputation, and glory. Let us flee all that could make us lose the grace of this holy and precious state we have. There must be no pretext, no excuse. Let us flee, let us flee creatures, if we desire to be united to Jesus. Their slightest breath is poison to us. O how delicate is the purity of the love of God! How small a thing stops it—and woe to the soul who opposes the holiness of its operations! Do not believe that it is easily communicated to every kind of person. No, no, we must be solitary, not only physically (for many people do this and live imperfectly), but rather, with the solitude of the heart which is nothing other than complete detachment.

Let us flee, then, from creatures, but flee still more from ourselves. Let us flee our moods, our inclinations, our own thoughts, our desires, our affections; let us flee from ourselves completely, as a disease which suffocates divine love in us; let us flee our reasoning and our own mind; let us flee our senses, and I testify at the feet of the Lord that we will find Him in fullness. He will give Himself to us without reserve and we will have no more reason to complain of our darkness, our powerlessness, and our poverty.

XX

Our Holy Father St. Benedict's spiritual affinity with the divine Eucharist[54]

I CAN ONLY ADMIRE ceaselessly the adorable providence of a God infinitely wise in His actions, for having chosen the religious of the great Patriarch St. Benedict to make them Daughters of the Most Holy Sacrament of the Altar. He destined them not only to render Him continual homage there, but also to be the Guardians of the sacred deposit He entrusted to His Church. It seems to me that there is a mystery in the choice God made of the children of this great saint; but I am not surprised, for although it is in some way incomprehensible, profound, and hidden, the way of life this great man had on earth and which he inspired in his disciples has a great affinity with the divine Eucharist, which I am convinced is the portion and inheritance of the Religious of St. Benedict. However, I am surprised that so many centuries passed without the children of that blessed father having entered into possession of the infinite bounty which God granted them.

If you ask me, my Sisters, what my reasoning is based on, I dare to assure you that it is a secret I discovered in the death of our most illustrious Patriarch, who, wanting to demonstrate his love for the Most Holy Sacrament of the Altar, could not render it more honor, nor show his faith and love in a more striking way, than to die in Its holy presence and give

---

[54] See Appendix 2 for commentary on this chapter.

111

the last beats of his heart to that adorable Host, enclosed in the sacred ciborium, in order to produce, in time, from the children of his Order, even until the end of the world, those who would give the Holy Eucharist adoration, reverence, the duties of love, and continual reparation. Yes! It belongs to the children of that glorious father to have a unique focus on this divine mystery, and also to have a likeness to it which is not common to other religious orders in the Church. For, if someone adores Jesus Christ in the various states of His holy life, can I not then say that the Religious of St. Benedict— who, according to the opinion of an excellent man of the last century, have the title of those who are dead—by their condition and state of death will honor, by relation and affinity, Jesus in a state of death in the Eucharist? The Fathers teach us that this is so in some way.[55] A child of St. Benedict, living a life of death, does he not have a connection and a likeness to Jesus in the Host? If I could be more specific about what the spirit and dispositions of a true Benedictine are, you would be convinced that by the faithful practice of the Holy Rule, she would have all the qualities of a Host and that she would enter into an admirable likeness to Jesus in the Holy Eucharist.

---

[55] According to St. Thomas Aquinas, the Lord of glory present under the consecrated species is the Christ-who-suffered, *Christus passus*. In the *Commentary on John*, he writes: "Since this sacrament is of the Lord's Passion, it contains within itself Christ who suffered. Hence whatever is an effect of the Lord's Passion is wholly contained in this sacrament, for it is nothing else than the application of the Lord's Passion to us. . . . Hence it is clear that the destruction of death, which Christ accomplished by his death, and the restoration of life, which he accomplished by his resurrection, are effects of this sacrament" (*Super Ioan.* 6, lec. 6, §964; cf. *In IV Sent.*, d. 8, q. 1, a. 2, qa. 2; *ST* III, q. 66, a. 9, ad 5 and q. 73, a. 5, ad 2).

But without multiplying the proofs about a truth which seems to me to be undeniable, judge only from this, my Sisters, if it was not by a divine and eternal plan that we, being Religious of St. Benedict, should become Daughters of the Blessed Sacrament. And are we not indebted to our holy Lawgiver for this grace? He merited it for us, without doubt, at the moment of his death when he buried the last moments of his life in the Most Holy Sacrament. Was it not a token of the love he had for that sacred Mystery, as well as appearing to be a promise that until the end of the world his order would produce in the Church victims offered to the Holy Eucharist, and that, not only would they adore day and night, but they would try with all their power to be reparators of His glory so profaned by the wicked in this Sacrament of Love? Do you not see, Sisters, that St. Benedict dies standing up to show us that he breathed forth, with an effort of love, the holy Institute we profess? He conceives it in the Eucharist to be produced twelve centuries later!

Oh, my Sisters, how divine is our Institute! How many centuries was it hidden and buried with Jesus in the Host? How long was it in the sacred entrails of the immolated God? My Sisters, He was sanctifying both the Institute and the souls whom He wanted to call to it. Oh what wonderful things I see and such great consolation they give me! No, no, my Sisters, this was not at all the plan of a human mind; no creature ordered, instituted, or chose it. It is Jesus in the Host who received it from the heart of Saint Benedict, and I can state, my Sisters, that it was taken from no other place than the tabernacle where this great saint deposited it at the last instant of his life.

APPENDICES

APPENDIX 1

Commentary on Chapter XVIII

A Monk of Silverstream Priory

"Let all the hard and rugged paths by which we walk
towards God be set before him."
Rule, chapter LVIII

THE HARD AND RUGGED PATHS by which a novice walks
towards God are set before him in the Most Holy Sacrament
of the Altar. The novice has only to gaze upon the Sacred
Host to discover the true spirit of his vocation.

In finem dilexit. "Before the festival day of the Pasch, Jesus
knowing that his hour was come, that he should pass out of
this world to the Father: having loved his own who were in
the world, he loved them unto the end" (John 13:1). Showing
His "love unto the end," Jesus walked towards His Father
along the hard and rugged way of the Cross, leaving us the
adorable mysteries of His Body and Blood as the abiding
memorial of His Passion.

The true spirit of our Benedictine life, as set forth in chapter 7 of the Holy Rule, is one of participation in Our Lord's
Eucharistic *kenosis* (self-emptying). Compelled by an excess of
divine pity, it was not enough for Christ to become for our
sake "obedient unto death, even death on a cross" (Philippians 2:8); He chose to perpetuate the *kenosis* of His passion,
even after His glorious resurrection and ascension into
heaven, in the adorable Sacrament of His Body and Blood.

In the Most Holy Sacrament of the Altar we find Our Lord

Jesus Christ in a condition of profound humiliation that, until His return in glory, announces the mystery of His death. "For as often as you shall eat this bread and drink the chalice, you shall shew the death of the Lord, until he come" (1 Corinthians 11:26).

The monk who contemplates the Sacred Host will, by the secret action of the Holy Ghost, come to resemble the One whom he contemplates. Mother Mectilde de Bar suggests that each soul is called to participate in some way in what she calls the states of Jesus the Host. The knowledge of each soul's particular correspondence to the Divine Host is, she says, given only in the light that comes from prayer. Once a soul has discerned what this correspondence is, she must pray for the grace to adhere to it by love, even though it be a hard and rugged thing to enter into the mystery of the *Christus passus* (Christ suffering).

It is Christ who gives one the courage to live faithfully in correspondence wih the states that are His in the Most Holy Sacrament of the Altar. It is He who prepares for each soul a particular way of relating to the Host; He applies it to the soul; He has already won for each soul the grace to enter fruitfully into correspondence with Himself in the various states of His sacramental presence.

What are these states? Writing in *Le véritable esprit* (*The True Spirit*), a spiritual handbook for her Benedictines, Mother Mectilde enumerates twenty-four of them. One must not, however, conclude that in her list of the twenty-four states of the Host, she has exhausted the diversity by which the Holy Ghost actualizes the infinite richness of Christ in the Church. Mother Mectilde offers her inventory of twenty-four states as a point of departure and as an indication of what the Holy Ghost may bring to light in each soul. "The Spirit breatheth where he will and thou hearest his voice: but thou knowest not whence he cometh and whither he goeth. So is every one that is born of the Spirit" (John 3:8).

> And there are diversities of ministries, but the same Lord. And there are diversities of operations, but the same God, who worketh all in all. And the manifestation of the Spirit is given to every man unto profit. To one indeed, by the Spirit, is given the word of wisdom: and to another, the word of knowledge, according to the same Spirit: to another, faith in the same spirit: to another, the grace of healing in one Spirit: to another the working of miracles: to another, prophecy: to another, the discerning of spirits: to another, diverse kinds of tongues: to another, interpretation of speeches. But all these things, one and the same Spirit worketh, dividing to every one according as he will. For as the body is one and hath many members; and all the members of the body, whereas they are many, yet are one body: so also is Christ. (1 Corinthians 12:5–12)

Here, then, are the twenty–four states of the Host that Mother Mectilde discovered; to each of them corresponds a virtue or fruit. Each state constitutes a particular form of holiness; a hard and rugged path to glory; a grace given for the upbuilding of the Church, and a participation in the priesthood and victimhood of Christ.

1. *Under the appearance of the Host, Jesus is the servant.* The fruit of correspondence to Jesus in His Eucharistic servanthood is *perfect charity.* "In this we have known the charity of God, because he hath laid down his life for us: and we ought to lay down our lives for the brethren" (1 John 3:16). "For which is greater, he that sitteth at table, or he that serveth? Is it not he that sitteth at table? But I am in the midst of you, as he that serveth" (Matthew 22:27).

2. *Under the appearance of the Host, Jesus is the victim immo-*

lated for sinners. The fruit of correspondence to Jesus in His immolation is *continual death*, according to the Apostle's word: "Always bearing about in our body the mortification of Jesus, that the life also of Jesus may be made manifest in our bodies. For we who live are always delivered unto death for Jesus' sake; that the life also of Jesus may be made manifest in our mortal flesh. So then death worketh in us, but life in you" (2 Corinthians 4:10–12).

3. *Under the appearance of the Host, Jesus is silent.* The fruit of correspondence to Jesus in His Eucharistic silence is *perfect silence.* "Jesus, for His part, was silent"; *Jesus autem tacebat* (Matthew 26:63). And the psalmist says, "Be still and see that I am God" (Psalm 45:11).

4. *Under the appearance of the Host, Jesus is, as it were, exiled and banished from His homeland.* The fruit of correspondence to Jesus in His Eucharistic sojourn is *pure love.* "Woe is me, that my sojourning is prolonged! I have dwelt with the inhabitants of Cedar. My soul hath been long a sojourner. With them that hated peace I was peaceable: when I spoke to them they fought against me without cause" (Psalm 119:5–7). Purified by much suffering, the Apostle says, "Charity rejoiceth not in iniquity, but rejoiceth with the truth; charity beareth all things, believeth all things, hopeth all things, endureth all things" (1 Corinthians 13:6–7).

5. *Under the appearance of the Host, Jesus is unrecognized.* "Verily thou art a hidden God, the God of Israel the saviour" (Isaias 45:15). The fruit of correspondence to Jesus unrecognized in the Most Holy Eucharist is *profound littleness.* "In that same hour, he rejoiced in the Holy Ghost, and said: I confess to thee, O Father, Lord of heaven and earth, because thou hast hidden these things from the wise and prudent, and hast revealed them to little ones. Yea, Father, for so it hath seemed good in thy sight" (Luke 10:21).

6. *Under the appearance of the Host, Jesus is contradicted and persecuted.* "Often have they fought against me from my youth, let Israel now say. Often have they fought against me from my youth: but they could not prevail over me. The wicked have wrought upon my back: they have lengthened their iniquity" (Psalm 128:1–3). The fruit of correspondence to Jesus contradicted and persecuted in the Most Holy Eucharist is *invincible patience*.

7. *Under the appearance of the Host, Jesus is powerless.* The fruit of correspondence to the powerlessness of Jesus in the Most Holy Eucharist is *perfect submission*. "Naked came I out of my mother's womb, and naked shall I return thither: the Lord gave, and the Lord hath taken away: as it hath pleased the Lord so is it done: blessed be the name of the Lord" (Job 1:21). And the psalmist prays: "But be thou, O my soul, subject to God: for from him is my patience. For he is my God and my saviour: he is my helper, I shall not be moved" (Psalm 61:6–7).

8. *Under the appearance of the Host, Jesus is forsaken and neglected,* even as it is written: "Despised, and the most abject of men, a man of sorrows, and acquainted with infirmity: and his look was as it were hidden and despised, whereupon we esteemed him not" (Isaias 53:3). The fruit of correspondence to Jesus forsaken and neglected in the Most Holy Eucharist is *flight from creatures*.

9. *Under the appearance of the Host, Jesus is consumed* in such a way that the Sacred Species cease to exist. The fruit of correspondence to the destruction of the Sacred Species is *the destruction of the old man,* according to Saint Paul's words: "Put off, according to former conversation, the old man, who is corrupted according to the desire of error. And be renewed in the spirit of your mind: and put on the new man, who according to God is created in justice and holiness of truth" (Ephesians 4:22–24).

10. *Under the appearance of the Host, Jesus makes expiation,* being, as it were, a penitent, not in the sense of having had to repent of any sin, for He is, as we say in the Roman Canon, "the Pure Victim, the Holy Victim, the Spotless Victim," but in the sense of being entirely turned toward His Father as the New Adam making perfect reparation for all mankind. "Him, who knew no sin," says the Apostle, "God hath made sin for us, that we might be made the justice of God in him" (2 Corinthians 5:21). The fruit of correspondence to this reparation of Jesus in the Most Holy Eucharist is *penitence in a spirit of reparation.*

11. *Under the appearance of the Host, Jesus is exposed to the power of His enemies.* The fruit of correspondence to the exposure of Jesus in the Most Holy Eucharist to His enemies is *perseverance in suffering.* Concerning this, Saint Paul writes: "There was given me a sting of my flesh, an angel of Satan, to buffet me. For which thing thrice I besought the Lord, that it might depart from me. And he said to me: My grace is sufficient for thee; for power is made perfect in infirmity. Gladly therefore will I glory in my infirmities, that the power of Christ may dwell in me. For which cause I please myself in my infirmities, in reproaches, in necessities, in persecutions, in distresses, for Christ. For when I am weak, then am I powerful" (2 Corinthians 12:7–10).

12. *Under the appearance of the Host, Jesus is abandoned to His Father's Providence.* The fruit of correspondence to Jesus' abandonment to His Father's Providence in the Most Holy Eucharist is *total abandonment to Divine Providence.* "Be not solicitous therefore, saying, What shall we eat: or what shall we drink, or wherewith shall we be clothed? For after all these things do the heathens seek. For your Father knoweth that you have need of all these things. Seek ye therefore first the kingdom of God, and his justice, and all these things shall be added unto you" (Matthew 6:31–33).

13. *Under the appearance of the Host, Jesus suffers the outrages and wicked treatment of sinners.* The fruit of correspondence to Jesus suffering the outrages and wicked treatment of sinners in the Most Holy Eucharist is the *humble acceptance of suffering.* "Who then shall separate us from the love of Christ? Shall tribulation? or distress? or famine? or nakedness? or danger? or persecution? or the sword? (As it is written: For thy sake we are put to death all the day long. We are accounted as sheep for the slaughter.) But in all these things we overcome, because of him that hath loved us" (Romans 8:35–37).

14. *Under the appearance of the Host, Jesus is poor.* The fruit of correspondence to the poverty of Jesus in the Most Holy Eucharist is *poverty in spirit.* "And opening his mouth, he taught them, saying: Blessed are the poor in spirit: for theirs is the kingdom of heaven" (Matthew 5:2–3), and again, "Yet one thing is wanting to thee: sell all whatever thou hast, and give to the poor, and thou shalt have treasure in heaven: and come, follow me" (Luke 18:22).

15. *Under the appearance of the Host, Jesus is as one buried.* The fruit of correspondence to the burial of Jesus in the Most Holy Eucharist is *a supreme indifference to changing things and an abiding repose in God.* "In peace in the selfsame I will sleep, and I will rest: for thou, O Lord, singularly hast settled me in hope" (Psalm 4:9–10).

16. *Under the appearance of the Host, Jesus is as one annihilated.* The fruit of correspondence to the annihilation of Jesus in the Most Holy Eucharist is a *descent into nothingness before God,* according to the word of the holy prophet Job, "I am brought to nothing: as a wind thou hast taken away my desire: and my prosperity hath passed away like a cloud" (Job 30:15).

17. *Under the appearance of the Host, Jesus renders sovereign homage to the holiness of God.* The fruit of correspondence to

the holiness of Jesus in the Most Holy Eucharist is *purity of life*. The prophet Isaias bears witness to this state:

> And I said: Woe is me, because I have held my peace; because I am a man of unclean lips, and I dwell in the midst of a people that hath unclean lips, and I have seen with my eyes the King the Lord of hosts. And one of the seraphims flew to me, and in his hand was a live coal, which he had taken with the tongs off the altar. And he touched my mouth, and said: Behold this hath touched thy lips, and thy iniquities shall be taken away, and thy sin shall be cleansed. (Isaias 6:5–7)

18. *Under the appearance of the Host, Jesus is hidden.* The fruit of correspondence to the hiddenness of Jesus in the Most Holy Eucharist is an *entire forgetfulness of self.* This the Apostle teaches, saying, "Mind the things that are above, not the things that are upon the earth. For you are dead; and your life is hid with Christ in God" (Colossians 3:2–3).

19. *Under the appearance of the Host, Jesus is a prisoner of love.* The fruit of correspondence to the enclosure of Jesus in the Most Holy Eucharist is *captivity of the senses*. Saint Paul says, "For this is the will of God, your sanctification; that you should abstain from fornication; that every one of you should know how to possess his vessel in sanctification and honour: not in the passion of lust, like the Gentiles that know not God. . . . For God hath not called us unto uncleanness, but unto sanctification" (1 Thessalonians 3–5, 7).

20. *Under the appearance of the Host, Jesus is solitary.* The fruit of correspondence to the solitude of Jesus in the Most Holy Eucharist is a *profound solitude*. "Therefore, behold I will allure her, and will lead her into the wilderness: and I will speak to her heart" (Osee 2:14). "And it came to pass in those days, that he went out into a mountain to pray, and he passed the whole night in the prayer of God" (Luke 6:12).

21. *Under the appearance of the Host, Jesus is all purity and centred in God alone.* The fruit of correspondence to the purity of Jesus in the Most Holy Eucharist is the *faithful reference of all things to God.* "Purge out the old leaven, that you may be a new paste, as you are unleavened. For Christ our Pasch is sacrificed. Therefore let us feast, not with the old leaven, nor with the leaven of malice and wickedness; but with the unleavened bread of sincerity and truth" (1 Corinthians 5:7–8).

22. *Under the appearance of the Host, Jesus is as one estranged among the wicked.* The fruit of correspondence to the estrangement of Jesus in the Most Holy Eucharist is the *loss of oneself.* "If any man come to me, and hate not his father, and mother, and wife, and children, and brethren, and sisters, yea and his own life also, he cannot be my disciple. And whosoever doth not carry his cross and come after me, cannot be my disciple" (Luke 14:26–27).

23. *Under the appearance of the Host, Jesus is obedient.* The fruit of correspondence to the obedience of Jesus in the Most Holy Eucharist is *trusting obedience.* In the Most Holy Sacrament of the Altar, Jesus is obedient to the commandment that He Himself gave to His Apostles: "And taking bread, he gave thanks, and brake; and gave to them, saying: This is my body, which is given for you. Do this for a commemoration of me. In like manner the chalice also, after he had supped, saying: This is the chalice, the new testament in my blood, which shall be shed for you" (Luke 22:19–20).

24. *Under the appearance of the Host, Jesus is held captive.* The fruit of correspondence to the captivity of Jesus in the Most Holy Eucharist is *the captivity of one's whole self in a spirit of sacrifice.* "But Jesus he delivered up to their will" (Luke 23:25). "For if thou hadst desired sacrifice, I would indeed have given it: with burnt offerings thou wilt not be delighted.

A sacrifice to God is an afflicted spirit: a contrite and humbled heart, O God, thou wilt not despise" (Psalm 50:18–19).

APPENDIX 2

Commentary on Chapter XX

A Monk of Silverstream Priory

IN THE FINAL CHAPTER of *The True Spirit*, Mother Mectilde offers her readers a sublime piece of writing and, at the same time, certain passages are hard to understand without entering into the seventeenth-century Benedictine's mind, and into her vast spiritual culture, shaped principally by the liturgy, Sacred Scripture, the Rule of Saint Benedict, and her many exchanges with other God–seeking souls of *le grand siècle*.

> I cannot help but admire ceaselessly the adorable Providence of a God who is infinitely wise and ineffable in His conduct, for having chosen religious of the great Patriarch Saint Benedict to make of them daughters of the Most Holy Sacrament of the Altar, and for having destined them not only to render Him continual homages, but also to be the guardians of this sacred deposit that He has entrusted to His Church.

Mother Mectilde ponders and admires the adorable Providence of God in choosing children of Saint Benedict to become in the Church perpetual adorers and guardians of the adorable mystery of the Most Holy Sacrament of the Altar.

Mother Mectilde's reference to Divine Providence is characteristic of her approach to all of life. For Mother Mectilde, the Providence of God is the mystery sung in the great O Antiphon of December 17th: *O Sapientia . . . attingens a fine usque ad finem, fortiter suaviterque disponens omnia*—"O Wisdom, stretching from end to end, mightily and sweetly ordering all things." Mother Mectilde read all of history in the light of Divine Providence; in this same light she read the twists and turns of her own personal history.

One of the most encouraging things about the lifelong journey of Catherine Mectilde de Bar is that she was often obliged to leave one place for another, to begin afresh, and to adapt to new circumstances. Again and again she experienced change, always keeping her heart fixed where true joys are found: in the adorable Sacrament of the Altar. For me, Mother Mectilde is the model of what the Church asks in the Collect of the Fourth Sunday after Easter:

> *Deus, qui fidelium mentes unius efficis voluntatis, da populis tuis id amare quod praecipis, id desiderare quod promittis: ut inter mundanas varietates ibi nostra fixa sint corda, ubi vera sunt gaudia.*

> O God, who makest the minds of the faithful to be of one will, grant to Thy people to love that which Thou commandest and desire that which Thou dost promise; that so, among the changing things of this world, our hearts may be set where true joys are to be found.

Trust and Perseverance

In times of social upheaval and unrest, as in times of upheaval and unrest in the Church, such as many of us lived through in the 1960s and '70s, the ideal of monastic stability is often shattered against the jagged rocks of reality. Happily, God calls a man not to an ideal, but to utter trust in Him and to humble perseverance in the face of things as they are— imperfect, gritty, and disappointing—even if this means beginning afresh over and over again. For me, Catherine Mectilde de Bar is a model of just this. God can and does, in fact, use such paradoxical and disconcerting circumstances as a crucible in which he hammers out something new, something purified, something conceived in the infinite love and wisdom of His Heart.

The Humble and Costly Yes

There are those who, judging the twists and turns of another's life through the lens of their own limited experience and prejudices, see only discontinuity where God sees, rather, the continuity of a humble and costly "yes," repeated again and again, to the unfolding of His plan. For the one engaged in such a circuitous and unconventional journey, there will be the subtle but cruel humiliations of the raised eyebrow, the sceptical glance, and the whispered (or not so whispered) critical inference. Religious types can be pitiless when it comes to such things. By God's providence, Mother Mectilde was surrounded, not only by critics and naysayers, but also by supportive and faithful friends who believed in her vocation and made sacrifices in order for her work, Our Lord's work, to prosper.

The Victimhood of Christ

Behind Mother Mectilde's text there shines the luminous word of Saint Paul: "For as often as you shall eat this bread, and drink the chalice, you shall shew the death of the Lord, until he come" (1 Corinthians 11:26). The Most Holy Eucharist proclaims the death of the Lord—the mystery of the *Christus passus*, Christ as victim—and makes present His Sacrifice from age to age, and this until the consummation of the world. Mother Mectilde could not, I think, speak of the Most Holy Sacrament of the Altar without hearing deep in the memory of her heart the words uttered daily at the altar in the Canon of the Mass: *hostiam puram, hostiam sanctam, hostiam immaculatam*, "a pure victim, a holy victim, a spotless victim." Mother Mectilde's understanding of the victimal character of the Christian life derives from the liturgy; it is articulated in the liturgy; it is lived through the liturgy. Mother Mectilde's approach to the monastic life is, I think, a classic example of the theological axiom: *lex orandi, lex credendi, lex vivendi.*

> But I glimpse the reason of the mystery of this choice and of the election that God has made of the children of this great Patriarch, and for this I am not at all astonished; because, although there is something incomprehensible, hidden, and profound in the state [of life] that this glorious Patriarch brought to the earth, and that he inspired in his sons, we see that it has so great a relation to the Divine Eucharist that I cannot but say that it is the portion and heritage of the religious of Saint Benedict. I should, rather, be astonished that it took the passage of so many centuries before the children of this Blessed Father quickened themselves to enter into possession of the inestimable treasure that the infinite bounty of God held in reserve for them.

A Mystical Affinity with the Most Holy Sacrament

Why did God choose Benedictines to enter deeply into the adorable Mystery of Faith and to become, in these latter centuries of the Church, souls entirely dedicated and configured to Christ in the Sacrament of His Love? Mother Mectilde, quoting Psalm 15, identifies the Most Holy Eucharist as the portion and heritage of the children of Saint Benedict: "The Lord is the portion of my inheritance and of my cup" (Psalm 15:5). She attributes this divine election of the children of Saint Benedict to a mystical affinity with the Most Holy Sacrament that pertains to their very state of life.

> If you ask me . . . where I get that which I have just said, I dare assure you that it is a secret which was shown me

in the death of our most illustrious Patriarch, who, wanting to witness to the love he had for the Most Holy Sacrament of the Altar, could do it no better than by expiring in His Holy Presence, thereby rendering the last breaths of his heart to this adorable Host, and enclosing his sentiments in the sacred ciborium, so as to produce, in time, children of His Order who would, until the end of the world, offer the adorable Host adoration, respect, and the bounden duties of continual love and reparation.

Mother Mectilde alludes to the death of Saint Benedict as recounted by Saint Gregory the Great in the Second Book of *The Dialogues*:

Six days before he died, he gave orders for his tomb to be opened. Almost immediately he was seized with a violent fever that rapidly wasted his remaining energy. Each day his condition grew worse until finally, on the sixth day, he had his disciples carry him into the chapel where he received the Body and Blood of our Lord to gain strength for his approaching end. Then, supporting his weakened body on the arms of his brethren, he stood with his hands raised to heaven and, as he prayed, breathed his last.

Configured to Jesus in His Death

There is in this passage something at once subtle and profound. In writing of the death of Saint Benedict, Mother Mectilde evokes the death of the Crucified Jesus. Both Our Lord and His servant, Saint Benedict, die with uplifted arms. Both die in an exhalation of love that will bring forth fruit, fruit that will remain (cf. John 15:16). Is not the "inclined head" of Jesus, noted in John 19:30, the key to understanding the summit of the Twelve Steps of Humility in chapter 7 of the Holy Rule?

131

Cum ergo accepisset Jesus acetum, dixit: Consummatum est. Et inclinato capite tradidit spiritum. (John 19:30)

"That is to say that whether he is at the Work of God, in the oratory, in the monastery, in the garden, on the road, in the fields or anywhere else, and whether sitting, walking or standing, he should always have his head bowed" (Rule of Saint Benedict 7:65). Does this not signify the complete configuration of the monk to Jesus in the mystery of His death on the Cross?

A New but Organic Development of Benedictine Life

Enlightened by a particular grace, Mother Mectilde perceives a secret: it is that Saint Benedict, in his last breath, exhaled a new but organic development in life according to his Rule: an expression of Benedictine life that would surround the august Sacrament of the Altar with adorers, vowed to repair by love the offenses, outrages, coldness, irreverence, and indifference suffered by Love living in the Most Holy Eucharist. This is, I think, a prophetic episode, akin to the prophetic actions of the Old Testament by which God announced, in figures and in types, mysteries that the prophets themselves could not yet see in their fulfilment. Again, this "secret" or "mystery" cannot be dissociated from the words that Mother Mectilde heard daily at the end of Holy Mass in the Prologue of Saint John:

> *In mundo erat, et mundus per ipsum factus est, et mundus eum non cognovit. In propria venit, et sui eum non receperunt.*

> He was in the world, and the world was made by Him, and the world knew Him not. He came unto his own, and His own received Him not. (John 1:10–11)

Mother Mectilde goes on to say:

132

Whereas some adore Jesus Christ in the various states of His holy life, the religious of Saint Benedict bear the title of those who are dead: this is what the blessed Monsieur de Condren, general of the Oratory, says. And so, cannot I say that their state and condition of being dead honours, by reference and relation, Jesus dead in the Eucharist? The Fathers teach us that He is there as one in the state of death. A child of Saint Benedict, living a life that is death, has he not a bond and a reference to Jesus in the Host?[1]

Hid with Christ in God

Here Mother Mectilde alludes, I think, to the impressive rites of Monastic Profession and Consecration with the prostration of the newly professed during the Holy Mysteries, and the use of the black funeral pall. This is another example of the principle of *lex orandi* that we find throughout the writings of Mother Mectilde. The Mother alludes also to Monsieur de Condren's characterization of the Benedictine grace as being one of death in the Pauline sense of the term:

> Therefore, if you be risen with Christ, seek the things that are above; where Christ is sitting at the right hand of God: Mind the things that are above, not the things that are upon the earth. For you are dead; and your life is hid with Christ in God. When Christ shall appear, who is your life, then you also shall appear with Him in glory. (Colossians 3:1–4)

Abandonment to the Father

In what sense exactly does Mother Mectilde speak here of Jesus being "dead in the Eucharist"? And in what way is the

---

[1] The text translated here is from a variant MS of *The True Spirit*.

Benedictine, like Jesus in the Host, in a state of death? The death to which Mother Mectilde refers is that of the *Christus Passus* in the Holy Sacrifice of the Mass and in the adorable Sacrament of the Altar.

In the Most Holy Eucharist, sacrament and sacrifice, Jesus Christ is present in the very act of His self-offering to the Father. The moment of death recorded by Saint John—"Jesus therefore, when he had taken the vinegar, said: It is consummated. And bowing his head, he gave up the ghost" (John 19:30)—remains eternally present to the Father in the sanctuary of heaven, even as it is present sacramentally in the Mystery of the Most Holy Eucharist. Jesus is on the altar, in the soul of the communicant, and in the tabernacle as He is heaven: the *hostia perpetua*.

The Benedictine enters into the death and victimhood of Jesus by allowing Him to renew at every moment in the sanctuary of his soul the grace of His head bowed in death that signifies complete abandonment to the Father. For Mother Mectilde this goes to the very heart of the Benedictine vocation: obedience (*Rule*, chapter 5), silence (*Rule*, chapter 6), humility, and the love of God, which being made perfect, casts out fear (*Rule*, chapter 7). It is precisely in these chapters of the Holy Rule that Mother Mectilde found what she calls "the true spirit" of her Institute:

> If it were permitted me to relate in detail the spirit and dispositions that a Benedictine ought to have, you would see that by the faithful practice of the Holy Rule, she would be altogether like a Host, and would enter into wonderful relations with Jesus in the adorable Eucharist.

Altogether like a Host

Mother Mectilde compares the Benedictine monk to the Eucharistic Host at two levels. The first level pertains to the qualities of the Host and the Benedictine virtues: the Host is hidden in the tabernacle, and the monk is hidden in the enclosure of the monastery; the Host is silent, and the monk is silent; the Host has no movement in and of itself, the monk has no movement that is not made by obedience; the Host is abandoned to the will of another, the monk is abandoned to the will of God mediated by his abbot. The Host is, to all appearances, powerless, fragile, and perishable; the monk, too, is powerless, fragile, and perishable. The hiddenness of the Host veils the glory of the Godhead. The silence of the Host befits the ineffability of the Word. The apparent inertia of the Host conceals the love that moves the stars: Dante's *amor che move il sole e l'altre stelle*. The abandonment of the Host into the hands of the one who picks it up—be he saint or sinner—reveals the vulnerability of the Word made flesh obedient unto death. It is in owning his powerlessness, his fragility, and his perishable flesh, that the monk experiences the power, the strength, and the imperishable life of the risen and ascended Christ.

The Monk: A Victim with Christ

The second level of comparison with the Host pertains to the victimhood of Jesus. The monk offers himself, by the grace of the Holy Ghost, to immolation on the altar in the Holy Sacrifice. There, Christ the Priest offers the monk, together with Himself, to the Father: a single victim (the very meaning of the word *hostia*) of adoration, thanksgiving, reparation, and supplication. Mother Mectilde would have been thoroughly familiar with the Preface of the Most Blessed Sacrament that was in use in Paris in the seventeenth century, which says: *Et nos, unam secum hostiam effectos…*

> In this mystery of unsearchable wisdom and boundless love, being Himself the One Who offers and the Vic-

tim, He ever wondrously effects what he accomplished once on the Cross. Making us one victim with Himself, He invites us to the sacred banquet in which He, our Food, is eaten, the memory of His Passion is renewed, the soul is filled with grace and a pledge of future glory is given. (Gallican Preface of the Most Blessed Sacrament)

In the altar, the Host, the Chalice, and the Cross, the monk reads the terms of his own immolation.

But, leaving aside a multitude of proofs that would confirm you in the truth that I am proposing to you, judge . . . if it was not by a choice all divine that we, religious of Saint Benedict, have become daughters of the Sacrament? And do we not owe this grace to the great Saint Benedict, who merited it for us by his precious death, as we have said? Was not his death the pledge of the love which he bore towards this sacred Mystery . . . the promise that, in the latter centuries, his Order would produce in the Church victims immolated to this august Sacrament, who would not only adore by day and by night, but who would be, insofar as possible, the reparators of His glory profaned by the wicked in the Sacrament of Love?

Saint Benedict's Eucharistic Grace

For Mother Mectilde de Bar, it is fitting that, of all the Orders that adorn the Church with their varied charisms, that of adoration and reparation belongs preeminently to the children of Saint Benedict. Mother Mectilde sees in Saint Benedict's wholly Eucharistic death—which, according to tradition, and in the learned opinion of Blessed Ildephonsus Cardinal Schuster, took place on Maundy Thursday—an unmistakable sign that his Order was destined, by divine election, to generate adorers and reparators of the Most Blessed Sacrament, and this until the end of time.

> Do you not see, my daughters, that Saint Benedict dies standing up, so that we might understand that he exhales, with the effort of love, the sacred Institute that we profess? He conceives it in the Eucharist, to be produced more than twelve hundred years later!

The Principle of a Wholly Eucharistic Life

Saint Benedict dies standing up. He dies before the altar. His last breath is an exhalation of fruitful love given in exchange for the Holy Viaticum of the final journey. He receives the Bread of Life from the Father and from the Church, and surrenders the breath of life into the hands of the Father that it might become, in future generations, the principle of a wholly Eucharistic life among his sons and daughters in the Church.

> Oh, my sisters, how divine is our Institute? For how many centuries was it hidden and buried with Jesus in the Host? For how long was it in the sacred entrails of a God-made-sacrament? He was sanctifying . . . both the Institute and the souls that He wished to call to it. Oh, what admirable things do I see and what consolation they give me!
>
> No, no, my sisters, this was not at all the plan of a human spirit, it was not a human creature that ordered, instituted, and chose this: it is Jesus in the Host who received it from the heart of Saint Benedict; and I can say, my sisters, that it was taken from no other place than the Tabernacle wherein this great saint deposited it at the last instant of his life.

A Quickening of Eucharistic Devotion

Mother Mectilde sees a quickening of Eucharistic devotion among the children of Saint Benedict as a treasure held in trust until, after the passage of many centuries, it emerged from its obscurity, like a Host brought forth from the tabernacle, to warm and vivify a Benedictine Order grown old and sterile, cold and dry.

> Oh, what a marvel that God should have entrusted this work to the most unworthy, not of Saint Benedict's children, but to one born out of time! To a soul who had neither the spirit nor the grace to do it! To a poor creature who had nothing remarkable except that she was of all creatures on earth the most criminal, and the one who had most profaned this august Mystery! God chose this sinner to serve as the most common and abject of instruments for so excellent a task, and to confound thereby the human spirit that loses itself when it sees accomplishments of this sort! This was done by a God. Nothing can be said except that one must prostrate oneself very low, and fear that, after having made use of this wicked instrument, He should cast it without recourse into hell.[2]

A Benedictine Not of the Classic Stamp

Mother Mectilde is conscious that her status as a properly professed Benedictine was called into question by certain hair-splitting canonists of her own time. She was, after all, a member of the Order of the Annunciation before making profession as a Benedictine at the monastery of Rambervillers on July 2, 1639. Even as a Benedictine, her life was character-

---

[2] Translated from the variant MS. Some of these sentences are missing from the MS used for the body of this book.

ized more by uncertainty and wandering from place to place than by the security and stability enjoyed by Benedictines of a more classic stamp.

> Gladly therefore will I glory in my infirmities, that the power of Christ may dwell in me. For which cause I please myself in my infirmities, in reproaches, in necessities, in persecutions, in distresses, for Christ. For when I am weak, then am I powerful. (2 Corinthians 12:9–10)

Mother Mectilde admits to being, like Saint Paul the Apostle, a child born out of time. She is, nonetheless, a true daughter of Saint Benedict, entrusted with a holy mission that transcended, by far, her natural capacities. She confesses to being the most common and abject of instruments, but cannot deny that she was the object of a divine election. Admitting this, she prostrates herself before the Divine Majesty and, following the counsel of her father Saint Benedict in chapter 4 of the Holy Rule, fears hell. The Mectildian-Benedictine charism is, I would suggest, even more necessary today than in seventeenth-century France when it rose up like a torch lifted high to illumine what Pope John Paul II called "the Eucharistic Face of Christ."